Crypto Revolution

Your Guide to the Future of Money

Written By

Bryce Paul & Aaron Malone

```Disclaimer: This book is presented solely for educational and entertainment purposes. The author, publisher and their respective affiliates are not offering it as legal, investment, or other professional services advice. All investment/ financial opinions expressed by the author are from personal research and experience and are intended as informational material. While best efforts have been used in preparing this book, the author and publisher make no representations or warranties of any kind and assume no liabilities of any kind with respect to the accuracy or completeness of the contents and specifically disclaim any implied warranties of merchantability or fitness of use for a particular purpose. Neither the author nor the publisher shall be held liable or responsible to any person or entity with respect to any loss or incidental or consequential damages caused, or alleged to have been caused, directly or indirectly, by the information contained herein. Any use of this information is at your own risk```

You should not treat any opinion expressed in this book as a specific inducement to make a particular investment or follow a particular strategy, but only as an expression of opinion. You should be aware of the real risk of loss in following any strategy or investment discussed in this book. Before acting on the information in this book, you should consider whether it is suitable for your particular
```

This book is dedicated to all the people who dream of making the world a better place than they found it.

circumstances and strongly consider seeking advice from your own financial or investment advisor.

All material appearing in the book/guides ("content") is protected by copyright under U.S. Copyright laws and is the property of CryptNation or the party credited as the provider of the content. You may not copy, reproduce, distribute, publish, display, perform, modify, create derivative works, transmit, or in any way exploit any such content, nor may you distribute any part of this content over any network, including a local area network, sell or offer it for sale, or use such content to construct any kind of database.

Table of Contents

Section 01

01

Welcome to The Crypto Revolution

There are countless stories of people who have been burned by "slow money". From racing against the clock and failing to get the money to stop a foreclosure, to running out of time when the only way to pay for an important medical procedure is cash, most people understand that when you need your money right away, if you look to banks and traditional currency, you're never going to make it.

In fact, these heartbreaking and infuriating stories are the driving force behind the CRYPTO 101 Podcast and the writing of this book.

We have spoken to an extraordinary number of people who have told us that "there has to be a better way". And in this book you will learn every compelling argument we know for investing in crypto right now.

This knowledge will empower you to become a citizen of Cryptnation…a true Crypto Crusader.

A Crypto Crusader is someone who stands for taking power back from greedy corporations, inefficient governments and the slow banks.

Yet you should be warned: **It is not an easy journey.**

Joining the Crypto Revolution requires a fundamental shift in how you view your responsibility towards money. The current financial system has all kinds of safety nets that crypto doesn't. And in return for these safety nets, *we hand over the keys to our financial lives*. Holding on to those keys with crypto requires an added level of responsibility.

Yet as you will learn, the positive upsides are, for the right person, absolutely liberating. Moving into crypto gives you access to an entire financial universe that is *not* dictated and controlled by governments, corporations and banks. And that's just the start.

This is why there are very powerful people who *do not* want crypto to succeed. Yet just like Napster and the music industry, by the time these powerful people and their institutions caught on, it was already too late.

Cryptocurrency is brand new technology that exists in a financial universe of its own. And it's for everyone.

Which means for you, it's not too late. You didn't miss the crypto wave. And the book you are holding in your hand will give you the security, hope and confidence to buy into the revolution, hold onto your crypto and become a Crypto Crusader. So that when the future does arrive, you'll be ready for it.

02

Who This Book Is For?

As told by Bryce...

Before I learned about Bitcoin and developed a burning passion for all things crypto, I wasn't exactly a tech geek. But after interviewing the smartest people in tech and studying all about blockchain technology and cryptography, I've pieced it together.

When the average person thinks about crypto, they probably think about getting rich quick and crypto millionaires. Although these situations do exist in the space, what really makes me excited is the technology.

That's why it took me so long to actually make my first investment in Bitcoin. I wanted to know everything I could about it first.

I think that reason, above all others, is why the podcast CRYPTO 101 has seen success. There is no doubt about it:

the technology that powers cryptocurrency is complicated. However, my focus is on breaking it down into simple terms so anyone can understand it.

This book continues in that same vein. If you are looking for complex equations, theorems and code blocks, this isn't the book for you. This isn't the book that will allow you to launch your own token tomorrow.

Instead, the goals of this book are simple:

To prove that crypto is more alive than ever, and that the odds are overwhelmingly in favor of mass adoption.

Most people interested in learning about future technology heard about Bitcoin long before it reached $19,000. They had many signs and opportunities, yet they failed to pull the trigger and generate life-changing wealth.

This book is not about "crypto lambos" and overnight millions. Yet the simple fact is that those who prepare for new technology will have opportunities to benefit massively from that preparation.

Just like your opportunities in the past, this book is a sign urging you to prepare for the future. Whether you listen or not is entirely up to you.

This book makes the case for cryptography. The backbone that the most major, innovative future technology is built on.

Cryptocurrency is the currency of cryptography. This book illustrates the different cases that show how the expansion of cryptography and cryptocurrency go hand in hand.

If you find my arguments convincing, the later sections of this book will guide you by the hand in joining the Crypto Revolution yourself. We are still in the "wild west" phase of cryptocurrency and I know you will find this book a trusty aid for getting in without losing your shirt.

Over the years, I've been asked by many people people WHY and HOW to get into crypto. I always wished I had a book to give them that would take them by the hand and guide them through it, step-by-step.

This is that book.

The book I'd give to Tracy, the girl who I met at a conference who asked me how to set up her own account.

The book I'd give to Celeste, my next-door neighbor.

The book I'd give to my grandma.

* Feel free to share the link to buy this book for someone you know: *cryptorevolution.com*

DISCLAIMER: Due to the nature of this book, we will be offering our predictions and personal opinions where appropriate. Although we've met with dozens of top experts in the field, please do not take our word for gospel. We are not licensed to provide investment advice. Use this book as the start of your research and exploration into crypto–not as the end.

03

Your Companion to This Book

We wrote this book to include everything you need to get started with crypto, and catch the next bull run safely.

This info is as current as it can be in a space that changes extremely quickly—even overnight.

If you would like to see our coin recommendations, as well as follow our trades step-by-step, visit this website for the book's companion group: crypto101insider.com

04

The Greatest Wealth Equalizer In The History Of Mankind

"Be greedy when others are fearful, and fearful when others are greedy."
-Warren Buffett

As told by Aaron...

Do you feel financially secure? If not, you are far from alone. In fact, only 28% of Americans consider themselves financially secure.[1] And the problem seems to be getting worse, even as the stock market reaches record all-time highs.

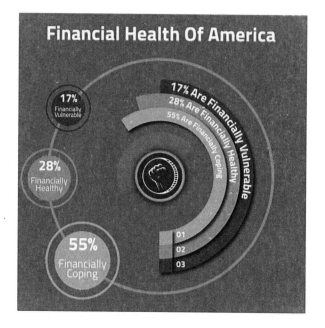

Financial Health Of America

17% Financially Vulnerable

28% Financially Healthy

55% Financially Coping

17% Are Financially Vulnerable
28% Are Financially Healthy
55% Are Financially Coping

01
02
03

How is this possible? Well, massive wealth is being made in the markets, but mostly by an ever-shrinking group of out of touch "elites." The top 0.1% of the richest people in the world own over 15% of the world's total wealth.[2]

And it's getting harder and harder to get a piece of it. Most people have no clue how to genuinely raise their income and status. The traditional methods of doing so, going to college and working hard, leads the average graduate to start out in the "real world" with student loan debt averaging $37,172.[3]

So, I have a question for you: How would you like a fresh start?

Between 2009 and 2019, millions of people did exactly that. Not by investing in stocks, playing the lottery, or starting a business, but by buying a simple cryptocurrency when the price was below $1.

That cryptocurrency was called Bitcoin.

In December of 2017, the price of a single Bitcoin shot up to $19,783.21.[4] This means if you had bought 100 Bitcoins for just $100 in 2011, your portfolio would've been worth $1,978,000 in 2017.

Now, at the current time, the price of Bitcoin has gone down a bit. The price hit a low of $3,122.28 in December 2018, and rebounded to about $14,000 in June 2019. Needless to say, the 2017 "bubble" has caused millions of people to pull their hair out, wishing they could go back in time to place an investment *before* the bubble burst.

Weary, they figured they just weren't lucky enough, so they dismissed Bitcoin, and moved on with their lives.

Having been involved in crypto for years, I know thousands of investors, ranging from people who bought in 2009 to people who bought in 2019.

Some poured hundreds of thousands of dollars in crypto investments, while others dabbled, investing small amounts like $50-$100.

And you know what? The people I get emails from who are panicking and worried about the price of Bitcoin are not the big spenders, also known as "whales." They're not the people who have lost over $1,000,000 in the current bear market. No, the people who are the most worried are the people who have invested, and know the least.

Meanwhile, my wealthy friends whose crypto portfolios are down, couldn't be more excited. In fact, many of them continue to double down, or dollar-cost-average their investment, meaning they are continuing to buy more and more coins.

While the everyday investor is screaming "Bitcoin is dead," the wealthiest investors treat a bear market like the greatest Cyber Monday sale of all time. They buy and buy. No talking head on TV or YouTube pessimist can stop them.

There's another group of people who aren't worried about bear markets: the developers. *Blockchain developers are busier today than they have ever been.* And as you'll soon learn, blockchain and cryptocurrency go hand-in-hand. The two share a "blood bond" of technology: the trust-free, or "trustless" ledger. Blockchain *enables* cryptocurrency.

They remember when the world said that Bitcoin would *never* be worth more than $0.50 a token. They look at the price today and they see monumental, history-changing progress. And although Bitcoin is, at the time of this writing, the world's most popular cryptocurrency, it's only the beginning. As you'll soon learn, the implications of cryptocurrency have already changed the world forever. And the best news of all? It isn't too late to join the revolution and become a Crusader.

05

The Madness of Crowds

"Men, it has been well said, think in herds; it will be seen that they go mad in herds, while they only recover their senses slowly, one by one."
- Charles Mackay

As told by Aaron...

In the 1600s, a man named Carolus Clusius made a discovery that would change the world forever.

Did he discover a cure for a devastating disease? Find a new country? Create a new invention? Nope. Carolus Clusius invented a new technique for growing tulips.[5]

Specifically, how to grow them in the low countries of the Netherlands—regions with harsh climates opposed to the flower's survival.

Before his discovery, tulips could only be grown in warmer climates like the ones in countries like Turkey. So almost none of the Dutch owned them.

Now, at the same time Clusius made his discovery, Holland attained its independence. And trade with other nations was flourishing.

So, what did Holland's citizens spend their new found wealth on? Status symbols. And due to the vivid, unmatched petal color of the tulips, the flower became a must-own for the rich and powerful members of society.

Although Clusius made growing tulips far easier for the Dutch, the flowers still took seven years to mature. This created an inherent scarcity that drove their prices even higher.

Then, as luck would have it, the tulips contracted a non-lethal virus.

Called the "Tulip Breaking" virus, it caused the tulip petals to "flame out" into multiple colors. As these new rare, beautiful tulips arrived, the prices skyrocketed, turning the buyer's market into a frenzy.

Inexperienced investors began trading tulips to make quick profits. In order to make profits even during the off-season, merchants invented contracts that investors could use to buy tulips before they were even in the store.

At the height of the tulip craze, *a single bulb could buy you an entire estate.*

Intelligent investors, realizing there was a divergence between the *price* of these tulips and the *value* of the tulips, stopped trading tulips, causing the demand to shrink. And then it happened: at a famous tulip auction, not a single bulb was sold. There was not a buyer in sight.

This created a panic in investors, leading them to sell their bulbs for a fraction of a price they could've fetched just days previously. The bubble was over, and thousands of people lost everything they had.

This was called "Tulip Mania", and its height lasted four years. From 1634-1637. [6]

The word "bubble" is used in financial and investment news all the time. Yet for hundreds of years, Tulip Mania remained the largest bubble in the history of the world. It was bigger than the "dot com" bubble of the early 2000s. And bigger than the real estate bubble of 2008.

Yet in 2017, Tulip Mania was finally overthrown. The award for the biggest bubble of all time would go to a brand-new champion.

Can you guess who finally overthrew the tulip bubble king?

It was Bitcoin.

What do tulips and Bitcoin have in common?

Think about it:

Absolutely nothing.

Yet both experienced massive bubbles for similar reasons. At the time, they were viewed as investments to get rich quick. For this reason, the price rose and fell *independent* of the inherent value of the flower or the currency.

This is about forgetting the bubbles and forgetting "get rich quick."

It's about pulling the curtain back from cryptocurrency to reveal what is actually happening in the industry. Because although much of the "hype" around Bitcoin has died down, the industry is more alive than ever before.

06

The Future is Crypto

As told by Bryce...

What most people don't realize is that when a massive Bitcoin bubble rose and burst in 2017, it injected a huge amount of capital into the industry. And while the media and naive investors have been more or less silent ever since, developers and companies in the space are absolutely thriving. Under the cover of media silence, most of the world's most profitable companies are investing in blockchain technology.

This book is about completely dropping the idea of using Bitcoin to "get rich quick." It's also about adopting the mindset of *preparing for an inevitable future.*

Ironically, when you drop the idea of "get rich quick", you are actually putting yourself in the perfect position to gain from cryptocurrency in the long-term. Gaining confidence and faith in the system will allow you to weather the storms of volatility that would scare away greedy, short-term thinkers and cause them to sell during a panic, or buy during a massive pump. You do not want to be that person. Remember the Warren Buffet quote at the beginning of Chapter 4?

That's why even though all the talking heads continue to be "skeptical" about crypto, I, as well as all the wealthiest, smartest investors I know *are still in the game, and continuing to increase our exposure to Bitcoin and other cryptocurrencies.*

For every person who got rich because they bought and held, thousands more fell for fake media fear and sold at the wrong times. While some got rich, they made zero or even lost all their money. They traded on greed and quick wins instead of embracing the future.

To succeed, they would've had to buy and hold...when the entire world was telling them to *run away as fast as they could.*

That's not easy.

Although the market forces and psychology that controlled Tulip and Bitcoin mania are the same, the underlying item being traded couldn't be more different.

No matter what someone is willing to pay for it, a tulip is still a tulip.

As you will soon find, the inherent value of cryptocurrency far exceeds that of fiat currency, and even precious metals like gold and silver. Have you heard the term fiat before? It certainly isn't an everyday term, but it *is* part of your everyday life.

A fiat currency is just the term for a government-backed currency—the $1s and $20s you hold in your wallet. But what does the term fiat really mean? Well fiat literally means "decree". The government is making a decree, or promise to the taxpayers that this fiat currency will always be redeemable for goods and services. You are betting on "the full faith and credit" of the issuing government. When has trusting a government promise ever ended spectacularly for us?

Fiat doesn't have any intrinsic commodity value like gold or silver, but it has been mandated into existence via regulations. It is only good as long as the government that issues it is "good for it". What happens when your country's credit rating (yes governments have credit ratings too!) is no longer good? They overextended their spending (of your tax dollars), they borrowed too much, they can't pay back their debts let alone keep up with the interest rates on those loans, and now they can't find another lender to keep up the facade.

Well its musical chairs at that point, and you don't want to be the one without a chair. The currency hyperinflates into oblivion because now there is no faith or credit to that government, and the dollars you've been saving lose all purchasing power. Many Latin Americans, for instance, have had to restart at zero after their country's currency collapsed. When the new government regime takes over, that government issues a new fiat currency. Some countries like Argentina have seen several currencies in a single generation, and each time a currency reset occurs, the value a citizen has stored in that fiat currency goes to zero. The higher the inflation, the more purchasing power the dollar loses over time. But by design, they are supposed to have "manageable" inflations.

Bitcoin, at launch, was worth $0. Bitcoin, in late 2017, was worth nearly $20,000. Do you see a trend unfolding here, one that is completely opposite of a fiat currency? Bitcoin started from absolutely nothing—didn't have a damn thing handed to it. It was given no help or mandate whatsoever from any corporation or government to use it. Rather, over time, citizens of *every* country elected Bitcoin. They chose to use it as their medium of exchange and store of value. When the Free Market was finally offered a choice in which money to transact in and store their hard-earned savings in, The People chose Bitcoin. This is directly reflected in its price. Soaring demand and limited supply have caused price to appreciate relative to the dollar and other assets. Bitcoin earned its value, and many other cryptocurrencies have too. Fiat currency cannot say the same.

Who knows where it will be in the future?

Yet none of these prices reflect the true value of cryptocurrency.

So how can you tell if a future technology will really change the world...or if it's just another tulip bubble? This book contains all the information I've learned after interviewing so many top experts in tech.

It was written to lift you out of the category of speculator and opportunist and put you in the rewarding category of a person who is prepared for the future *right before it happens*.

There are unstoppable forces you will soon learn about that are driving the crypto and blockchain movement. While the rest of the world is struggling against these forces, this book is an invitation to let them work in your favor.

Empowered by the knowledge that this future is coming, you'll have the chance to make smart investment choices. And while you may see gains in the short-term, you can rest easy knowing that as long as you hold, the inevitable forces of math and change will do the rest.

The form of money controls our lives. And better money will inevitably lead to exponentially better lives for all of us. This is the crucial statement I want you to get from this book. To really explain it, we need to start from the very beginning.

07

Artificial Intelligence

As told by Aaron...

"Go" is the name of an ancient Chinese game. Created 2,500 years ago, it's thought to be the oldest strategy game in the world.[23] It's also one of the most complicated. Due to the open, large size of its board, there are practically unlimited possibilities for openings and responses.

In China, some of the country's brightest children are exposed to Go at an early age. The ones that show promise are then trained practically from birth to play the game at the highest level possible.

Go is more complex than Chess.[8] In fact, due to the size of the board, there are more possible move combinations on Go than atoms in the known universe.

Which is probably why Artificial Intelligence was able to defeat a Chess grandmaster in 1996,[9] while being unable to defeat a Go grandmaster. Go players claimed that the game was simply too complicated and no machine could beat a true human master.

In 2016, AlphaGo, an AI developed by Google's Deepmind project, played legendary grandmaster Lee Sedol. AlphaGo won in convincing fashion, 4-1.[10] It wasn't just that AlphaGo won, though. It's *how* it won.

AlphaGo made moves that no human being had ever thought of, in one of the most studied board games of all time! Because of the winning moves made by AlphaGo, the entire strategy of Go has practically been rewritten, with the best players studying the AI's moves in depth.

AlphaGo went on to defeat 60 different grandmasters in rapid succession, posing as an online user named "Master."[11]

Following the success of AlphaGo, Deepmind decided to raise the stakes. They created a new version of AlphaGo, called AlphaGo Zero. But this time, the rules were different. AlphaGo Zero would receive no human input or guidance. Instead, it would be simply told the basic rules of the game. And it would learn from playing against itself.

In just three days, AlphaGo Zero defeated the AI version of AlphaGo that defeated Lee Sedol. Within 20 days, AlphaGo Zero could beat the AI that beat 60 grandmasters in succession. Entirely self-taught, AlphaGo Zero is now the greatest Go player to ever exist.

Three days. Three days to master the most complicated game in the world. 20 days to defeat the previous AI that was fed thousands of games from human masters. The AI revolution is already here. AI can learn how to perform human tasks and, overnight, perform them far better than the smartest humans to ever walk the Earth.

AI Thinks Differently Than We Do

In 2017, developers at the Facebook AI Research Lab created an AI chat program. They taught the program common English words and phrases, then they had the AI chat with itself.[12]

On checking their progress, developers were shocked to see the chat bots speaking in a language completely foreign to human beings. They'd created a brand new language and were now choosing to use it to communicate over English, as it was considerably more efficient for them.[13]

Word of the bot went viral with news stories sharing it far and wide. It was easy to see a sinister picture. Two chatbots talk to each other, develop their own language, and before we know it, end up taking over the entire world. In this case, the reality was that although the chat bots were deviating from their English script, the programs were still running within the bounds the developers had originally created.

What this story illustrates is that AI is not human. This may seem like an obvious point, but there are extremely important ramifications. For example, if AI requires a different language to communicate at maximum efficiency, could it also be possible that the same AI requires a new form of currency?

In this case, will it be easier for developers to change fiat money to fit in with AI, or use a natively digital currency built from the ground up for machines to work with? Or, will the AI create its own currency?

It's all possible with crypto–it's impossible with fiat. Just another reason why fiat currency is weakening and, although it may take time to happen, cryptocurrency will ultimately win out in the currency battle against government-sponsored fiat.

"Non-Work" Income Streams

The rapid advancement of AI has opened up the future, and companies like Google, Uber, Apple and Tesla are going "all in". One of the technologies that we'll all soon be using on a daily basis is self-driving vehicles.

These cars are *already* far better drivers than humans. Although accidents can still happen, they'll happen exponentially less when software is driving the vehicle. Letting machines do our driving for us will save millions of lives because most accidents are caused by human error and distraction. Autonomous vehicles will enable us to travel at much faster speeds, accomplish valuable tasks while commuting, get to locations faster, and greatly speed up logistics for transportation of goods and services.

So, where does cryptocurrency come into play here? It's simple: trust. Let me try to paint you a picture.

Right now, companies like Uber own the software to make ride-sharing possible and mainstream. Thousands of drivers all over the world are using the app to make money on the side. What will happen to these drivers when automation takes over? They'll be out of a job.

However, with cryptocurrency, they have another option. Uber is the largest taxi service in the world. Yet they don't own any of the vehicles that make money for them! Individuals do. Well, it's only a matter of time before autonomous cars become mainstream, and with cryptocurrency, those who are prepared can benefit, instead of worrying about lost jobs.

Individuals will be able to group together and buy an autonomous car themselves. The car owners will then be able to install open-source apps that connect your car with a marketplace of riders and other vehicles. Think of it exactly like Uber, without Uber taking a middleman cut because we won't need a centralized corporation to process payments!

Instead, the future is one of open networks where any rider can broadcast their location, any car can broadcast its location, and a sophisticated matching engine can connect the two.

When the car arrives, the rider will scan the car's QR code to unlock the car and start the ride (like we do with the publicly shared Bird Scooters now). Payment is sent to a smart contract that is coded to execute the payment when we arrive at the destination, or when the rider opts to end the ride. The fee is quickly calculated and automatically executed. Then, the money is immediately distributed to the digital wallets of everyone who has a stake of ownership in the car, based on the percentage they own! They can even let the car keep a balance in its digital wallet too, so that it can order its own repairs and recharge its battery!

Through cryptocurrency and smart contracts, this entire system can be automated, allowing everyday people countless new investment options to supplement their income. There is no need to fear automation if you already have a vision of the future in your mind and are prepared for the inevitable.

Simply by reading this book you are becoming aware of the possibilities that will be at hand. You will be so far ahead of the curve, you will be looking for investment opportunities that others *don't even know exist.*

By the time we collectively start to feel the overwhelming implications of automation, you will already have years of experience interacting with cryptocurrencies and the digital economy. Others will be fearful, but you will have knowledge. Fear exists only where knowledge lacks.

On a similar note, one of the hottest political terms right now is Universal Basic Income (UBI). This is the idea that every single person should receive a living allowance every single month. For example, every month, the government would mail you a check for $1,000. It's certainly not enough to live a life of luxury. However, it would potentially remove a huge chunk of financial stress from your life.

There are many different ways UBI could be implemented. Not only can UBI be put on a public, open blockchain to secure it and prevent fraud, the new income streams made possible by taking ownership *over* automation will allow every individual to have multiple "non-work" passive income streams.

Now, could these systems also be possible with current fiat currency and technology? Yes, but it'll have to be controlled by a middleman. You will still have to trust a third-party not to get hacked, and you'll still have to trust that the government and federal reserve won't inflate the currency or diminish the value of it through zero or negative interest rates.

Where trust in humans is required, corruption breeds, and the hard-working taxpayers always foot the bill whether they know it or not! It's just not fair, and that is why Bitcoin was originally invented: To pose an alternative to the current status quo.

The famous President Ronald Regan quote comes to mind here: "Trust. Then verify." In the case of cryptocurrencies, there is no *trust* ever needed because the blockchain mathematically *verifies* everything the moment a transaction is sent and settled. That's why some have begun to refer to blockchain as a trust or truth machine.

For a disgusting example of how a few corrupt individuals can cripple a nation, look no further than the pharmaceutical industry. Companies like Purdue bragged internally that their new opiate Oxycontin would lead to a "blizzard of prescriptions."[14] Meanwhile, they told doctors that their new drugs wouldn't lead to addiction.

Finally, when it turned out that OxyContin *did* lead to mass addiction, the company blamed patients.[15] Meanwhile, Purdue raked in billions of dollars in profit. The same kind of corruption present in the hearts of big bankers caused the subprime mortgage bubble and subsequent collapse of the housing market.

But *removing trust from money* isn't just about avoiding corruption.

Human beings conquered the world in large part due to our ability to perceive, process and understand data. We are data-generating machines. Every time we step outside of our homes, we're measuring data on the environment. How many cars are on the street. What the weather is like. How we're personally feeling (if we're well or sick). The number of people we spot wearing the color green.

On top of that, there are a lot of experiences we go through as individuals that generate a ton of precious data. For example, if, God forbid, you come down with a serious disease like cancer, that is a goldmine of data. You spend tens of thousands of dollars on treatments that analyze everything about your body. But due to HIPAA and other privacy laws, that data will stay behind closed doors. It's a good system that, for the most part, protects patients.

Facebook and Google are both free services, yet they're some of the most profitable companies in the world. How? Because of *our* data—the data we generate by using their services—gets analyzed, sorted, packaged up, and sold. Because of how we use both of these platforms, advertisers have profiles on who we are, and what we're most likely to buy. They can then target us with ultra-specific advertisements that are dialed in to as close to how we feel in that moment as possible.

So, here's the question: who really owns *your* data?

This is one of the most hotly debated topics in today's society. Many of the companies that make fortunes off of curating, selling and trading our data don't do so with our express permission. Sure, they have a lengthy terms of service that would take days and thousands of dollars in lawyer fees to understand. Meanwhile, they are reaping in billions in profit. At some point in the very near future, it's going to come to a head.

In the future, everyone could have their own privately-owned identity on the blockchain. Just like with cryptocurrency, you would have a public and private key. This means you—and only you—would have access to this data.

When you log into a site, instead of saying "Log in with Google" or "Log in with Facebook", you will log in with your private key, which will securely and privately hold all the elements of your digital identity. Today we use our digital identity more than we could possibly imagine, across almost every app, service or device that we use. Your digital identity is made up of everything you do online, and is owned and controlled by third-parties.

This will make it virtually impossible to be hacked without your express permission, unless someone steals your private keys.

You can use your blockchain identity to sell your data on an open marketplace. If Google and Facebook are interested in making money off of your data, they can pay you an agreed-upon fee for doing so. Every time you "like" a funny cat picture or look something up, you could be paid for doing so.

Walking around the city, you could collect valuable data that the city would benefit from. If you went through an expensive medical treatment, you could sell your private data from that treatment back to the hospital and researchers.

Do you see where I'm going with this? Due to terms and conditions being so vague, and people being naive to how their data is being used, it actually hurts both parties.

On one hand, you never know who has your data or how they're using it. On the other hand, laws like HIPAA make it impossible for doctors and health researchers to get patient data on a large scale that could be used to drastically improve their services and potentially even cure major diseases.

With identity on the blockchain, individuals can specifically choose who uses their data, how their data is used, and actually get paid for sharing it.

Crypto companies are already coming out with these kinds of "non-work" income streams. With automation and the creation of more "non-work" income streams, cryptocurrencies are vital to achieving a true state of abundance for every human being on Earth.

Did you know you can loan out crypto and earn passive interest like a bank? It's just one of many new "non-work" income crypto is making possible today. To learn more, visit crypto101insider.com

Interplanetary Species

AI and the technologies of tomorrow will help improve the quality of life for every single person on Earth.[16] Yet we'll still be at the mercy of the planet we live on. It's possible that all this new abundance will bring about a massive increase in population. Although, current trends show that the more developed a country is, the more stabilized and lower the birth rate is.[17] It's still a problem to be wary of.

At the same time, in the vast universe, we're sitting ducks. At any time, a large asteroid could move into a collision course with Earth. Any number of cosmic events could happen that upset the fragile balance of life. For these two reasons, and more, humanity has always looked toward the stars.

Further development of space technology will allow us to mine valuable resources from asteroids and other planets. Terraforming technology could help us turn the surface of planets like Mars into potentially more hospitable environments.[18]

Today we have dozens of well-funded private companies working on taking humanity to the stars. Elon Musk, the founder of SpaceX, has his sights on Mars. His goal is to have human beings land on Mars by 2025.[19] A vocal supporter of cryptocurrency, Musk has famously said "paper money is going away."[20] With space exploration and travel moving from government control to the private sector, Bitcoin, or a similar public, borderless, permissionless, immutable, fixed-supply crypto network could be used to transfer value and settle debts through space at the speed of light.

08

Slaves to Money

"I believe that banking institutions are more dangerous to our liberties than standing armies. If the American people ever allow private banks to control the issue of their currency, first by inflation, then by deflation, the banks and corporations that will grow up around (these banks) will deprive the people of all property until their children wake up homeless on the continent their fathers conquered."
-Thomas Jefferson

As told by Bryce...

Well folks, Thomas Jefferson's worst nightmare came true. A private bank is in control of the issue, or issuance, of our currency. The Federal Reserve is a privately owned company and it controls the issuance—or printing—of our money.

Straight from their website: although an instrument of the US Government, the Federal Reserve System considers itself "an independent central bank because its monetary policy decisions do not have to be approved by the President or anyone else in the executive or legislative branches of government, it does not receive funding appropriated by Congress, and the terms of the members of the board of governors span multiple presidential and congressional terms."

To understand the importance of cryptocurrency in your life, you have to come to terms with this simple fact: your freedom...your right to happiness...was stolen decades ago by people who are no longer on this Earth.

Sound dramatic?

To give you the full picture, we first need to talk about money. The following is a basic explanation on how money works, and why what the government decides to do with money affects you on a personal level.

Money exists as a form of convenience. Back in our primitive days, we were focused solely on our survival. Survival meant having adequate shelter, enough food and water, etc. It took constant work to survive, and the accumulation of resources needed for survival was very valuable.

Let's say we're living back in primitive days. You go out and kill a deer. I go out and I'm not able to kill a deer. My survival is threatened. On the other hand, it rained while I was out hunting and the water catcher I invented is full to the brim. You weren't so lucky, and are running short on water.

Based on what we were each able to get for ourselves, we can trade. You could offer me some of the deer meat in exchange for some water. We both agree on the terms of the deal (i.e. how much water should you get for how much deer). We both get what we need to survive. It's a fair trade.

However, as humanity evolved, transactions got more complex and involved more parties, so barter became less viable. Through investment and innovation, I might have developed a way to collect 100x the amount of water during a rainstorm. However, I didn't need 100x the amount of deer, or any other good in return for the water I was collecting.

No. I wanted to preserve the value that I produced so that I could buy a big plot of land, and the materials necessary to build a house. Moreover, I couldn't use deer meat to store the value because that deer meat would go bad over time!

So, a medium of exchange had to be invented. Something that could *represent* an agreed-upon value of goods or services at a given point in time that could be redeemed in the future for the same amount of value.

Now, let's get back to the origin of money.

When humans decided to create something that represented value, they realized it had to be special. It had to retain its value. Using the home-selling example, a person would only be willing to sell their home for a pile of rare seashells if they knew those seashells would be worth just as much the next day.

And not every medium of exchange is capable of holding its value. Apples will only stay fresh for a small period of time. Something more durable like a metal is capable of lasting much longer. Therefore, if all I have to trade with is apples, and you have copper coins, you are going to be much more wealthy than I can ever be.

In this way, we are faced with the key point of this chapter: *currencies go to war with each other*. The stronger the currency...the longer it lasts...the better it stores value...and the easier it can be exchanged for something else...the more likely that currency will win out.

This battle waged for ages, vacillating from seashells to rai stones to diamonds to silver to salt...with one durable, unique, and rare material generally winning out: gold. It became the currency and debt settlement layer that our entire world was built upon.

Gold is particularly strong, and was unanimously and universally chosen as money for many reasons. Here are three of the biggest:

1. **It's durable**

    Due to the chemical stability of gold, it's very difficult to destroy or degrade it. Gold lasts millions of years in the same state, and can even survive harsh environments like being left in the ocean for hundreds of years.

2. **It can't be replicated**

    Gold is, so far, impossible to replicate. Many have tried, all have failed.

3. **It's finite**

    There is only a finite amount of gold available on the Earth, and mining it costs enormous energy, effort, and risk. Something valuable means that thing is very hard to produce and is very scarce.

If everyone had it or could get it easily, it wouldn't be valuable.

With the widespread adoption of a form of money like gold, something remarkable happened: our *time preference* shifted.

Having a money like gold *lowers* our time preference, meaning it incentivizes us to delay gratification and plan for our futures—*saving*.

On the contrary, having a money like paper fiat currencies is, in principle, like a game of hot-potato. Get rid of it as quick as possible, since by design a dollar today is worth *more* than a dollar tomorrow—*spending*! Weak currencies, like paper fiat, heighten our time preference, meaning they incentivize us toward instant gratification because it's difficult to trust that they will still hold equal value and acceptance years down the line.

In our primitive years, our only goal was to survive and replicate. The best way to survive in a life-or-death situation is to focus all of your energy on the present. What can you do *right now* to make sure you live another day?

This is the kind of thinking that drives a dog to follow you around everywhere you go, begging for food. It wants to survive, and it knows the best way to do so is to *eat something right now*...even if they just ate!

This kind of mindset works for base survival. However, it is the antithesis to growth and long-term prosperity. That's because quite often, short-term decisions are actually bad for the long-term.

This is something that is scientifically provable, and everyone instinctively understands because we've all experienced it! For example, in today's society, there's no end to junk food. And our bodies crave it almost constantly. Yet the best option to live a long, healthy life is to avoid junk food and instead, go to the grocery store and make something healthy at home.

The invention of strong currencies allowed human beings to shift into long-term thinking: now that we could be confident our wealth would still be around 10-20 years into the future, we could start to *benefit* from long-term planning.

Strong currency broke us out of the primitive cycle of survival and permanently shifted us into a species that could grow and flourish.

And grow we did. Using a long-term, low time preference mindset, we invented agricultural techniques that allowed us to cultivate and *store* massive quantities of food. We created complex distribution and logistics systems. The ability to achieve such scale further incentivized us to start families and produce as many offspring as possible to help with the work.

Important to note here is that the massive and impersonal corporations that we have globally today are a new construct relative to how long humans have been in existence. Prior to the 17th century, most businesses were purely family run operations.

Ultimately, low time preference caused us to create larger and larger societies. People eventually started to group together to address commonly shared issues and debate how these new cities and masses should be managed—thus, governments started to form. Over the centuries, governments were given increasing amounts of control over every aspect of human life, including how we transact and handle business with one another.

By the time large governments started to form, however, gold had already been in use by its citizens. This gave the government two options:

1. **Watchdog**–Use and safeguard a currency backed by a tangible, valuable substance, like gold.

2. **Despot**–Remove the tangible value from a currency and make its only backing the government itself.

The Fall of Rome

We can see how government interference in money affects a civilization by examining one of the most advanced civilizations to ever exist: Rome.

Founded in 27 BC, Rome created its strength through military conquest. The more wars won, the more resources Rome was able to collect, and the wealthier its citizenry became. With excess wealth came spending, and Rome became used to always having the income to justify its excess.

However, in the reign of Nero, between 54-68 AD, that was no longer the case. There were no resource-rich lands left to conquer. Yet the citizenry and government continued to spend. Instead of attacking the root problem head on, which would've led to massive unpopularity, Nero took the route that almost every government eventually defaults to: he hid it.

At the time, Rome had a strong currency that *always* contained 8 grams of precious metal per its most valuable coin. Nero's strategy was called "coin clipping", and it involved removing a small amount of precious metal from every coin in the empire.[21] Initially, nothing happened, and Rome was able to continue spending past its limit. However, this began a vicious cycle of inflation that grew worse and worse.

This caused future emperors to continue the devaluation of the currency. At a certain point, the price of basic goods became too high, and the economy started to grind to a halt. The emperors turned to totalitarianism, placing price controls on these goods. In other words, instead of being controlled by free market supply and demand, the government would set the price for goods like bread at a certain rate.

Of course, this did nothing to stop the problem, as now the market itself could no longer function. The great Roman empire crumbled.

Unlike in Rome, the creator of Bitcoin, Satoshi Nakamoto, built in a hard limit to the number of Bitcoins that can exist: 21,000,000. After this number of coins have been mined, no new coins can be created.[22] This eliminates the possibility of a third-party manipulating currency for their own selfish gains, while diluting the wealth and savings of a naive or uninformed public.

Currency Death Spiral

When money is a power that exists outside government influence, societies flourish. When governments intervene and take control, societies, no matter how great, spiral into destruction and death.

Although it's been a long time since Rome, we're currently faced with a far bigger financial crisis than the Romans ever were. And whether you're aware of it or not, you are a slave to it. It is sucking your life force and wealth and will continue to do so until the system implodes in on itself, devastating the lives of everyone who is plugged in.

Still think I'm being dramatic? Let's take a look at where we're at.

As powerful and large as the Roman Empire was at its peak, it pales in comparison to the largest empire of all time: The United States of America.

Like every great empire throughout history, the United States was built on a strong currency backed by gold.

A major blow to gold came in 1944 at the Bretton Woods meeting, when the U.S. dollar, in a roundabout way, became the de facto reserve currency of the world because the U.S. had the most gold in reserves.

Initially, the U.S. dollar was directly tied to the gold standard and dollars were redeemable for gold, but changes in the world economy forced the U.S. to completely divorce the dollar from the gold standard in 1971 [23] at the hands of Richard Nixon, long after inflation had started to accelerate.

But the general move away from gold started long before the official divorce in 1971. Fun Fact: did you know that in 1933 FDR's Executive Order 6102 made it ILLEGAL for citizens of America to hoard large large amounts of gold coins or bars. Why? The rationale was that hard times during the Great Depression had caused people to hoard gold, which stalled economic growth and made the depression worse.

Basically, this move was meant to allow the Federal Reserve to increase the money supply during the depression. At the time, the Federal Reserve Act required all cash that was issued by the Fed to be backed 40% by gold. So they could print $1.00 if there was only $0.40

worth of gold on reserve—a little thing called leverage, and this is how *credit* was invented!

By the late 1920s, right as the recession was upon us, the Federal Reserve all but reached the limit of allowable credit that they could issue, because they didn't have enough gold as collateral to issue any more cash. So they either needed the People's gold in order to expand the money supply, or they needed to reduce the Fractional Reserve requirements, which happened later. This was amended in 1974 by President Gerald Ford.

Fractional Reserve Lending

Although there are many different currencies in the world, because of the Bretton Woods agreement all currencies are tied to the US dollar. Similarly, the vast majority of financial institutions in the world run in the same way. And that is, by using Fractional Reserve Lending, or Fractional Reserve Banking.[24]

This concept is based on the fact that people deposit more money into the bank than they withdraw. So if you put $10,000 into your bank account, the bank only needs to keep a portion of that in reserve.

Because most people aren't withdrawing their entire savings, the banks will always be able to pay withdrawals with their total reserve stockpile. So what do they do with the other 90% of the cash? They loan it out. That way they can make all the money on the interest from those loans.

It's how banks work. If they couldn't loan out any of our money, they wouldn't be able to make money. When you deposit your money into a bank, you are actually loaning to them, and they pay you a super tiny, negligible bit of interest.

They are literally in the business of borrowing your money in order to loan it to someone else! We feel good because they keep our money safe, but we aren't necessarily getting a great deal! After all, they need us just as much as we need them, but that isn't being reflected in the deal terms!

For one thing, at any given moment, the bank could be spending your money on something you don't agree with. You'll never know about it...and you'll never get the choice. That's because as long as the bank can give you money from someone else's reserve, you'll never miss it.

As long as you can take your money out whenever you need, the system works, right? Well...not quite.

How "Normal" Banking Works

To explain the enormous problems caused by Fractional Reserve Banking, I need to tell you how banking works without it.

At any bank, an individual can make one of two types of deposits.

1. Demand

2. Time

A demand deposit is money that you want to be able to withdraw on-demand. So, if you put $10,000 into a bank account, you want to be able to access that money whenever you need to.[25]

A time deposit, on the other hand, is an investment. You invest in the bank for several months or years, intending to get a higher return when your money comes back.[26]

Without Fractional Reserve Banking, the only money a bank could use for loans would be time deposits. With Fractional Reserve Banking, the bank can use all the Time deposits, and roughly 90% of the demand deposits (subject to fluctuating government mandated Reserve Requirements).

So, What's The Problem?

First off, banks only make money based off your deposits, and you get hopefully a 1% interest on your deposits, if you are lucky. But the person borrowing your money via the bank's credit card has to pay 25% APR on the money they borrowed! The bank keeps the 24% and nets that as their profit, but they wouldn't be able to loan any money or have a business if it wasn't for customer deposits! And customers get 1%! The whole retail banking model takes advantage of the average consumer by not paying depositors a bigger, fairer share of interest earned.

Further, although both demand deposits and time deposits are similar, they affect the total world economy in completely different ways. This is because of interest rates set by the Fed.

Fractional Reserve Banking, on the other hand, consists of artificially low interest rates. This is because the practice of Fractional Reserve Banking is actually creating money out of thin air.

Let's say you deposit $10,000 into the bank. The bank then loans $9,000 out...while still showing you have $10,000! Essentially, they've created $9,000 new dollars from scratch and injected it into the economy.

Commercial banks can also get loans from the Federal Reserve, the U.S. "central bank", and again, only need to keep a fractional reserve.[27]

Because interest rates are artificially lowered, and not based on free market principles of supply and demand, there is a distortion in the *real* economy—low interest rates incentivize businesses to take on risky and potentially unsustainable investments. At the same time, the price of goods also goes up overall, because more "cheap money" is available.

Let's zoom in from the macroeconomic view we've been discussing to illustrate the debacle we find ourselves in, in more concrete terms. As mentioned, during times of easy money and expanded credit the economy experiences increased investment. (You might have heard of government subsidized "stimulus packages". It is a related concept in the Business Cycle where the government steps in to stimulate national economic growth and activity. These are typically emergency bailouts to save industries littered with "malinvestment".) It is only natural that some of those investments don't pan. The investment turns into a malinvestment, becoming completely worthless. For instance, an investment bank might buy equity in a software startup. That startup uses the money they just raised to pay salaries, conduct research and development, spend big on marketing, etc. If the startup goes bust, the investors lose their money. In times of "hard money" as opposed to "easy money", investors are less risky with their hard-to-come-by cash, and are forced to do deeper diligence and make sounder investments.

The vacillation between spending, investment, easy credit, and low interest rates vs. saving, hard credit, and high interest rates is known as the Debt Cycle, or the Business Cycle.

Quantitative Easing

The end result of all of the processes that have been discussed is the decline in purchasing power of your dollar. As the value of a currency depreciates, basic survival goods become more difficult and expensive to buy. This puts pressure on citizens to survive, who then put pressure on the government to improve their life situation.

Because the people running governments want to avoid this pressure, like Nero, they will make choices to "hide" the reality. One of the most dramatic ways modern governments do this is through a process called Quantitative Easing.

Quantitative Easing is a complicated word for printing money. The idea is that the more "cheap money" is available, the more people will take out loans. The more loans they take out, the more money gets circulated throughout the economy. So Quantitative Easing is a clever way of dripping fresh currency into the market.

Initially, this has the exact intended effect. People suddenly have more money available, so they spend more. This causes the price of goods to rise, until these loans need to be paid back. Because the money didn't come as a result of new value creation, and instead came as a result of printing it out of thin air, there's no money to pay off these loans.

Quantitative Easing provides the *illusion* that you are earning more value in return for your time. It also provides the illusion that the stock market is becoming more "valuable", when in fact money is just getting cheaper. Asset prices are denominated in dollars, and in this context, the long-term rise or "reflation" in asset prices is just a reflection of a weakening currency.

That's why even though the markets are higher than ever, not everyone feels it.[28] And many are in worse financial shape than they've ever been before.

Many economists argue that Quantitative Easing spared the USA from another Great Depression (similar to the tactics they used in the actual Great Depression to expand the credit in the system). In the short-term, it appears they were right. However, this graph of U.S. national debt tells another story:

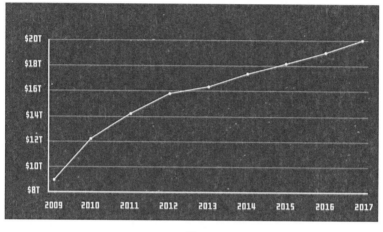

29

Everything has a cost, and the chickens are coming home to roost. The end result is inflation and dramatically increased public debt.

Because of these forces, the money you've worked hard your entire life to earn, is worth less than it should be.[30] Because a tiny handful of people who control the U.S. Dollar, and through it, the world, made certain decisions, you're left picking up the pieces. And although the economy remains in decent shape at this moment, it all could go south. Quickly.

Governments and despots always follow the same pattern. They need money RIGHT NOW. In order to get that money "for free", they create it by devaluing their currency. This causes inflation and creates a "debt" the public has to pay off. Ultimately, this can bankrupt a society, as was the case with Rome. In modern times, we've seen this happen to many countries including Argentina (twice!), Zimbabwe, and Venezuela. People had to restart from zero after their currencies became worthless.

We see a lot of parallels to America today. Although the truth is, if hyperinflation were to happen in America, it would be even worse, because the U.S. Dollar is the reserve currency for the entire world.

If not for one revolutionary invention in 2009, this would be a book about doom and gloom. Thanks to that one invention, though, it's the opposite.

With the Fed doubling down on money printing, many financially savvy investors are buying crypto. To learn how to use crypto to protect your savings from hyper-inflation, visit crypto101insider.com

09

Who Else Wants To Own A Bank?

As told by Bryce...

Cryptocurrency is called the "people's currency" for a reason. When crypto breaches the mainstream, the value of your money will no longer be decided by the financial elites.

First of all, you won't *need* a bank account at all. The costs for storing cryptocurrency are tiny. And you can bypass them by using a wallet, which are very secure now, and are quickly surpassing bank security levels (more on this later).

You could very easily use a "hot wallet" to pay for everyday goods and services. You could store your savings on a physical, offline "cold storage" device at a safe spot at home.

In the future, it's most likely there will be many different digital currencies, each with different uses. Later, we'll be talking about seven different industries that each have their own type of digital token right now.

So, it is possible that in the future, Fractional Reserve Banking and traditional structures will still exist in some form. But there's an incredibly important difference: it will become optional.

With a digital currency like Bitcoin, every transaction is on the open ledger. There are no secrets. And banks can't pretend to be storing your money while they're actually lending it out.

Even if you store your money with a third-party (which you won't need to do), you will be able to use your public key to check every single step your money takes. If that third-party is loaning out your money, you can check on that at any time.

**There are private blockchains owned by private companies, and privacy tokens that allow you to send private or proprietary transactions.

The banks won't be able to claim your money is safe when they are really investing it in high risk products...because you'll be able to see for yourself exactly where it's going.

Your money will have a digital paper trail on the blockchain.

Because of the open, connected, and transparent nature of blockchain databases, it makes risk analysis much more efficient and accurate. The bank and its regulators will be able to know exactly where their balance sheet risks lie, and make more accurate models to mitigate risk and catastrophe.

Blockchain can insure against another catastrophic failure of the banking system, like in 2008 when Lehman Brothers was leveraged 50:1 and essentially got margin called by its creditors (other banks) because over the weekend their market cap lost 2%. In one singular moment, the entire industry was faced with the simple fact that they were insolvent. They went bankrupt on that Monday and were sold for pennies on the dollar.

Please don't just take my word for it. In a speech by former SEC Commissioner Giancarlo on March 29th 2016, he says "If a blockchain record of all of Lehman's transactions had been available in 2008, then Lehman's regulators could have used data mining tools, smart contracts and other analytical applications to recognize anomalies…Regulators could have reacted sooner to Lehman's deteriorating creditworthiness."

This removes the artificial cash from the monetary system. And while there would still likely be market fluctuations, it would be due to the *actual economy*...not what a small number of bankers decide is a good way to make a profit and artificial interest rates.

In short, crypto provides a bulwark against predatory banking policies that cause inflation to rise too quickly and literally steal the value from the money you've worked so hard to save and store.

Also, due to the fact that many cryptocurrencies today have limited supply and are deflationary in nature like Bitcoin (only 21,000,000 Bitcoins will ever exist), a world run on crypto has even more safeguards against runaway inflation.

Make Money Like a Bank

In 2018, banks generated over $236 billion in profit for the year.[31] And that's profit! Which means it's the money that comes in *after* all salaries are paid. After all the end of year massive bonuses. After all the private jet flights, fancy meals, luxury hotels and exotic retreats. Hundreds of billions of dollars in pure profit.

How is it done? Loans and Fractional Reserve Banking. Because banks have such a streamlined system for loaning out money— even to people in "high risk" categories— they are able to print money at record levels year over year.

How would you like to do the same?

It's possible with crypto. Crypto unlocks stale, no-yield capital by opening up previously impossible investment opportunities.

Here's an example:

Let's say you have $10,000 in savings. If it's sitting in the bank, it's generating a tiny amount of interest. In a crypto world, let's say someone wants to buy a house for $100,000. Instead of getting a loan from a bank, the purchaser could borrow it from a community pool, or a "community bank" instead.

You could deposit your $10,000 of cryptocurrency in that decentralized bank, which is just a piece of open-source software (AKA smart contract) that programmatically fulfills the same function as a bank.

Maker DAO is one of many projects currently building such systems. Any number of other independent investors could come in add their money to the pooled funds. Using a smart contract, the percentage ownership of the house would be automatically, legally, divvied out. Since you loaned 10%, you own 10% of the house.

Also under the same smart contract, as the loan is paid back with interest, the person who bought the home increases their equity ownership. So, if the first month they pay back $10,000, at 4% interest, that's $400 in monthly income to you.

If you decided to lend to a high-risk borrower, you could be making 6%-8%. Although it might not sound like a ton of money, it's much higher than you can currently make with savings accounts. And even certificate of deposits and other investment vehicles. The more money you could invest, the more you could make on that money.

Combine this fact with the "non-work" income sources crypto will bring (which I'll discuss shortly), and financial freedom becomes a quick and guaranteed reality for people living where these systems exist. And since blockchain and crypto span worldwide...everyone will benefit.

10

Math Money

As told by Aaron...

One of the biggest critiques of cryptocurrency is that it "isn't backed by anything." Although I understand where this idea comes from, it couldn't be further from the truth.

Cryptocurrency isn't backed by *just* anything. It's backed by the strongest, most reliable force human beings have ever discovered: mathematics.

Cryptocurrency gets its name from cryptography, which is defined as "the art of writing or solving codes." One of these codes is called a "secure hashing algorithm", or SHA. Basically, a hashing algorithm will take a simple word or phrase and create an entirely one-of-a-kind alphanumeric footprint for the input.

Hashing is a way of compressing data, and hashes are used everywhere in blockchain systems. There are many different kinds of hash functions (MD5, SHA-1, SHA-256, etc.). In fact, SHA-256, the hash function securing Bitcoin, was developed by the NSA!

A hash function takes any amount of data and spits out a fixed-size value (i.e. SHA-256 always spits out a value that is 64-characters long). One-way hash functions, the variation that secure cryptocurrencies, are impossible to reverse engineer. This means that you can't derive the input value from the output value.

For instance the SHA-256 hash of the letter "a" is *always* going to output:
CA978112CA1BBDCAFAC231B39A23DC4DA786EFF8 147C4E72B9807785AFEE48BB

The sentence "Cryptocurrency is changing the world." when hashed is always going to be:
93BC4593A7D0D9DD949041982EFAF6AC155C63A405 86DEA4FDEC40C56DCDF3BD

However, if you remove the period from the sentence you will get a completely new hash value:
0BA7096FD4742AB21409E54904C2A788EE5D8DC4A4 9ED304FDE4DDD057929CF8

You can use SHA-256 to hash the text of an entire book and it will be compressed into 64 characters!

Another important quality of working hash functions is that they are *collision-resistant*, meaning that no two pieces of data that you hash will *ever* spit out the same output. If a collision is eventually found, that hash function is considered broken and it is retired in place of a new algorithm.

Hashing allows us to compare two pieces of data and infer if those two pieces of data are the same or not. If you hash two large pieces of data (like the 250GB Bitcoin blockchain, which is growing every day) and you get the same output, then you can trust that the input data is the exact same. You don't have to manually review the data to see if anything has been tampered with because the hash function already did it for you!

To put it into different terms, let's say you send out a legal contract. Prior to sending, you can run it through a hashing algorithm to get the hash value of the contract. When that person sends it back to you, you can rehash the contract they sent you. If the hashes don't match, you can be certain that the file was altered by that other party (even though the person might have said they didn't make any tweaks!).

So why are hashes useful in blockchain?

Hashes make it so that you don't have to trust anything other than Math, which is an unchangeable, constant force in nature.

In blockchain, hashes are used to represent the *current state* of a blockchain, from the very *first* transaction until now. The input to the hash function represents everything that has happened on that blockchain, every single transaction up to that point (think of it like hashing an entire book like in the example above).

This means the hash output is based on and therefore affected by, all previous transactions that have occurred on a blockchain. So, a bad guy trying to change any transaction that has previously happened on a blockchain would change all prior hashes, making those transactions easy to spot as fraudulent, and rejected by the system. This is because the blockchain is a transparent, open, publicly auditable database. Since *every* transaction must happen in plain view of the whole network, malicious or fraudulent transactions will be programmatically flagged and rejected by the other nodes running the blockchain, thus maintaining the integrity of the entire system.

The other aspect of cryptocurrency that relies heavily on math is your account information—your public keys and your private keys. Think of it like a username/email address and password.

Your private key is like the lock to your house or the password to your email. If anyone has it, they can take coins in that public address, which are protected by nothing other than your private key. You need your private key in order to send crypto to others, but most wallet apps keep this hidden from view and use the private key automatically in the background.

Non-custodial wallet apps are built so that they never see your private key. The only way you can regenerate your private key is via your 12 or 24 word recovery phrase, which you will be prompted to write down when you generate a wallet. Do NOT give it away to anyone. Do NOT post it on the internet for any reason, no matter who asks. It's yours and yours only. Do not lose it.

If you want to receive cryptocurrency from someone else, you will give them your public address so they know where to send it. Public addresses are pseudonymous, meaning that it represents you without revealing your identity. You will have many public wallet addresses as you dive deep into crypto.

Your public address is a *hashed* version of your public key. Because the public key is made up of a very long string of numbers, the hashing compresses it to form the public address. Basically, your private key generates the public key which, in turn, generates the public address.

Every crypto has its own public address. For example, you cannot send Litecoin to a ZCash address. You cannot receive Monero with your Bitcoin address. Here's an example of a Bitcoin public address:

38xFFKmQdY8Ax6e8Gfz4D7Wr9K1CVPUY1a

Again, think of this as you would an email address for your crypto. It is safe to give this to anyone. It looks like a string of random numbers and letters. Each cryptocurrency has its own parameters; the length of the key or the starting number/letter (for example, all Ethereum addresses start with 0x and most Bitcoin addresses start with the number 1 or 3).

Again, when using a wallet app that stores multiple cryptocurrencies, coins in that wallet use different addresses. Each cryptocurrency has its own wallet address, so be very careful.

When noting your public address always either copy and paste it or scan the QR code generated, never write it out manually to avoid making a mistake. If you send Bitcoin to an Ethereum address or make a mistake in the address name, it will be lost forever. Most good wallet software will have warnings and address validation security measures in place. But not all wallets have this, so don't send crypto when you're tired or drunk. Pay close attention. Please note, all ERC20-type tokens may use the same wallet address as your Ethereum address.

Even though the public addresses seem confusing now, take hope! There are inter-blockchain protocols being developed, like the FIO protocol from the Foundation of Interwallet Operability, which will give wallets human-readable addresses and many other abilities to make sending crypto as easy as sending an email.

11

Just How Secure Is Cryptocurrency?

As told by Bryce...

When it comes to finances, there is one point that's more important than any other: security. Is cryptocurrency 100% secure?

For as many decades as banks have had to develop security and anti-fraud measures, consumers lost almost $1.5 billion due to hacks and other frauds.[32] And the FTC reports that 17,000,000 people had their identity stolen in 2018.[33]

What would a world powered by cryptocurrency look like?

First, let's talk about how Bitcoin, the world's most popular cryptocurrency, handles security.

In upcoming chapters, I am going to teach you how to set up your first cryptocurrency wallet. This is where you'll store all the different tokens and coins you invest in.

When you create your wallet, you'll get a public and a private key. In order to access your wallet, a hacker would need both your public AND private key.

Provided you never tell ANYONE what your private key is (and this is rule #1 of crypto security), here are the steps a hacker would need to take to guess (or "brute force") your Bitcoin SHA-256 private key.

To put this in simple terms, there is currently not even enough compute power existing in the world to hack a Bitcoin private key. Let me paint you a fun picture of why we say crypto is secured by math.

First, the hacker would need access to a computer that is so powerful, it has 3x the power of every server Google owns put together. Google is estimated to have between 1,000,000-10,000,000 servers.[34]

One computer with the power of THREE GOOGLES put together.

Then, that hacker would need to create FOUR BILLION more of these computers.

At this point, the hacker would not have *anywhere near* the processing power to discover your private key, even if he ran those computers for *the entire lifespan of the discovered universe.*

Our hacker decides to get crazy.

He flies an enormous spaceship to four billion earth-sized planets. He then populates every single one of these planets with four billion of his super computers…each.

However, he's disappointed to learn that even with four billion planets running four billion supercomputers each, he still can't guess even one private key even if he had 13 billion years to run his computation.

For his final move, he visits four billion galaxies. In each of these galaxies, he gives four billion planets four billion supercomputers.

He then smiles to himself, satisfied. Because he now has a one in four billion chance of guessing a single private key in the entire lifespan of the discovered universe.

As you can see, although hacking or guessing one private key is mathematically *possible*, it's so improbable and difficult that for human purposes, it *is* impossible.

Now, there have been instances where crypto *exchanges* have been hacked. These are places that allow you to exchange one cryptocurrency for another. Their centralized servers have been compromised, employees leak information, or a bug gets found in their website that allows hackers to gain restricted access to the site. But banks have also been hacked. And the reason why banks don't get hacked as often today is because they've had decades and billions of dollars to figure out advanced security protocols.

In this way, you cannot say that fiat is inherently more secure than cryptocurrency. You can only say that the current fiat world has had more time to develop security. Given the same amount of time, or in reality, considerably less time, crypto exchanges will evolve even better security mechanisms.

The most compelling reasons for cryptocurrency come from outside of the system itself. There are unstoppable forces of nature that caused the birth of cryptocurrency. These same forces of nature are pushing against fiat...and moving the world towards inevitable widespread adoption.

Here are some of the other forces at play here:

Human Pain and Suffering

One of the main reasons crypto is so important to me is because *a global money moving at the speed of life can save lives.* The problems of fiat affect people at every single level of the emotional scale. From the inconveniences that come with a wire transfer going wrong, to not being able to receive life-saving treatment in time, money impacts every single level of our lives. In a way, it's good news. Because guess what? The better our money is, the better our lives will be.

Maybe nothing will improve the human condition more than making the switch from fiat to crypto. From a TRUST economy to a TRUSTLESS one.

Insurance For The U.S. Dollar

12

The New Gold Standard

As told by Bryce...

As we mentioned before, one of the biggest reasons why investors naysay Bitcoin is because it doesn't have anything "backing it." What they are really saying is that Bitcoin doesn't have any cash flows like a stock. It doesn't have any physical utility like gold or silver. It doesn't have any yield like a bond. And it doesn't have a government like cash.

While the above is true, the arguments are moot because Bitcoin was never designed to have any of those things. It was designed to be an entirely new asset class. If anything, the closest analog would be gold because gold doesn't have cash flows, yields, or a government behind it, but it does have utility outside of its use as an investment vehicle-mainly, every sophisticated electronic device has a small bit of gold in it for its unparalleled conductive properties, and resistance to corrosion.

So as a refresher, what makes gold inherently valuable?

- **Scarcity**–There is only ever a finite amount of gold on the planet. Once we mine it all, it's gone forever. Since at this moment, gold can't be copied or cloned like diamonds can, this gives gold an inherent value or "backing." This is why gold has, since the beginning of human society, been the currency of choice for the world's most powerful nations.

- **Resource Intensive**–The only way to get gold is to mine it. This requires an enormous amount of human effort and ingenuity. Although our Earth contains an abundance of gold, actually uncovering it from the depths of the planet is no easy task.

- **Usefulness**–Gold is an incredibly durable and pliable metal. From being used as a conductor in supercomputers to being worn around the neck to display status, gold has inherent usefulness.

Now, let's take a look at Bitcoin.

- **Scarcity**–As mentioned previously, there will only ever be 21,000,000 Bitcoins created. Just like gold,

Bitcoin has scarcity built-in.

- **Resource Intensive**–Bitcoin requires "pro work" to generate coins. This means that must use their compute power and expens to verify every single transaction that hap the Bitcoin blockchain.

- **Usefulness**–Blockchain technology, and t trusted third-parties, has almost unlimited applications in today's world (more on thi A borderless currency that requires no pe can be sent anywhere, at anytime, to anyo virtually zero cost is very useful. And, it killed if the entire internet is shut off!

Although Bitcoin is a digital currency, it shares same advantages that gold does.

Now you may be thinking, "Well Bryce, at least backed by physically minted dollars and coins."

But even that is far from the reality. In fact, The Electrical and Electronics Engineers reports that of total US dollar circulation is in paper or coins words, the other 90% is just numbers on bank s after creating loans AKA credit money.[35]

I get asked a lot when cryptocurrency is going to take over the world. To this I usually give two answers at once:

1. It already has

2. It doesn't need to

When Bitcoin was released, it was like opening Pandora's Box. Suddenly, a currency existed outside of the control of any one government or regulatory power. It had a clear value proposition and people slowly started to set up miners and bought into it.

Just like how the first social networks were developed in the 1990s, but we didn't have Facebook until 2008, Bitcoin is just the first iteration of something that will become so large and awe-inspiring we literally can't imagine it right now.

An analogy to help understand where we are would be that the early users of the internet could only send simple text files. Slowly, they could start uploading images, but they never dreamed of streaming live 4K Virtual Reality over a system that could only send a few kilobytes of info per second…yet here we are.

In the same way, people can't currently imagine the magnitude of possibilities that a programmable, global currency will unlock. The applications that will plug into and leverage crypto networks will change how we do business, transact with our friends, save, earn, and invest. Crypto will be powering all sorts of new applications, and by owning those cryptos, you own a piece of the network and applications built on top of it. Inherently, the more demand there is for the network and applications the more valuable they are, and that value is reflected in the market price of the cryptocurrency.

On the other hand, I'm in no rush for crypto to "take over." In fact, it won't need to. Simply stated, cryptocurrency is built on the most consistent natural force humanity has ever discovered: math.

It can't be corrupted by a tiny handful of minds at the very top. Because we're in the very early stages of digital currency, it's volatile. No one knows what's going to happen. But as more and more people plug into the system, the system will gain a level of stability that's impossible with the current fiat system.

So, at this point, it's a waiting game. No one knows what will happen to the U.S. dollar. And this isn't the book for speculation on financial crashes and horror stories in the future. But the fact of the matter is, cryptocurrency is our insurance—our digital gold standard—against the fiat currencies in the world

Bringing the World Online

And it's not just about the USA. That's what most people forget. People tell me that they're not sure if crypto will ever really "catch on" because the current money system works just fine. Maybe it does…in the First World.

Right now, there are 7.53 billion people living on planet Earth. Just one billion of those people live in the USA and other western developed countries.

Although life in the USA is fairly stable, other countries are not so lucky. Just look at Venezuela, for example. Dictator Nicolas Maduro has made one poor financial decision after another, absolutely crushing the value of the money of the Venezuelan people.[36] The end result? Riots, starvation and death.

The reason you are reading this book is because whether you know it or not, you have an entrepreneur's mindset. You're likely into cryptocurrency because it provides a potentially rapid and exponential return on your investment. Something you're unlikely to get in the stock market.

Well, there's another vehicle for investment you may not have heard of: developing countries.

More than 3 billion people live on less than $2.50 a day.[37] These people, for all intents and purposes, are "cut off" from you and I completely. That's because they don't have access to our financial system.

They can't open a bank account. They can't get paid in U.S. dollars. They can't invest in the stock market. And...*they can't take investments from other people.*

I'm living in San Diego, California right now. At any point in the day, I can take out my phone and order food from Uber Eats. Within minutes, it'll be waiting outside, ready for me to pick up and devour.

Go to rural Ethiopia and try doing the same thing. But the thing is...that demand is still there. What if you could join up with millions of other investors from First World countries and invest in an Ethiopian village?

Using Bitcoin, you could transfer money to the village's investment account through a smartphone. Using smart contracts to ensure work actually gets completed and returns are distributed to investors based on their percentage of ownership in the decentralized autonomous organization, you could help a group of villagers set up a food delivery system.

You and your fellow investors have now brought an entire village online! Not only will this work to eliminate poverty within that village, it will also bring a new productive workforce into the modern-day economy.

Millions of people in the poorest countries own cheap, durable smartphones.[38] With the power of cryptocurrency, these people can now use their simple phone for banking, credit/loans, and even global stock market investing!

Now, think of all the luxuries you have in your day-to-day life. And now realize that those were brought about primarily by the one billion people living in the developed world. In other words, our world is functioning as well as it is, utilizing less than 1/7th of its total productive power (i.e. human capital)!

Want to see exponential growth in your investments? Imagine being a real part of ending poverty and disease for the entire world. It's impossible with the current hyper-regulated, heavily-bordered, financial system.

With cryptocurrency, it's inevitable. Why? *Because that's where the money is.* Investors sick of getting small returns with bluechip stocks on the markets will be more than happy to invest in developing countries and watch as entire economies blast off. As these investments grow and begin to reap profits, the impact should spread to every corner of the world.

Within a matter of years, world poverty could be extinguished...and we could finally have the entire productive power of the human race online.

Foreign Remittances

There are currently 100 million immigrants working in western countries. Every year, they send $445 billion to their families at home. [39] These transactions take days to clear, and every time they send money home, they pay companies like Western Union up to 15% in transaction fees.

On top of paying taxes, these expensive transaction fees mean less money in their family's pockets. Although cryptocurrencies do have transaction fees, they are *significantly* less, and they clear within seconds. This allows immigrant workers to send more of their hard-earned money home, injecting more money into that local economy.

Savings

Saving money in the world's poorest countries is almost impossible. There is such a high risk of businesses, banks, and governments defaulting on their loans to the First World. This is because their currencies are extremely weak and volatile, their GDP is terrible, and therefore the interest rates they get on their loans are extremely high! This has a nasty trickle down effect to everyone who is a citizen of that struggling nation who can barely keep pace with interest payments! If your country defaults on its loans or a corrupt dictator takes over and fires up the printing press, hyperinflation inevitably follows, and economies collapse.

Cryptocurrency allows these people to tap into a much more secure global network of finance. For the first time in their lives, they'll be able to put money away for a rainy day in a currency that is not their own national currency, or anyone's national currency for that matter. They can put their savings into many *global* currencies.

Although this is just the tip of the iceberg, it's easy to see how cryptocurrency is going to transform the developing world, and bring everyone up to speed.

13

The Enemies of Crypto

As told by Bryce...

Not only is crypto potentially the biggest wealth transfer in the history of the world, it's also the biggest *power* transfer. Because right now, the people who control the banks control the money and the world. Whether these are good people or bad people isn't the question. Likely, the group consists of both.

And, this group is currently the most powerful group of people in the entire world.

Moreover, they may be the most powerful group of people to *ever exist in the history of the world.*

They control all the money.

And cryptocurrency is a direct threat to their way of life.

These behemoth institutions make billions of dollars controlling and managing the world's money. As soon as cryptocurrency reaches critical mass, the bulk of what they do is no longer needed. Whether or not good people work at the institution, the institution desires to survive. No one wants to lose their job.

And so the Crypto Revolution faces the toughest, wealthiest and most capable enemy of all time: the big banks.

Ever since Satoshi released Bitcoin's whitepaper in 2008, the banks have been hard at work discrediting Bitcoin, blockchain and cryptocurrency.

- Hedge Fund Manager Ray Dalio has called crypto a "bubble."[40]

- Economist and New York Times writer Paul Krugman has gone as far as to call Bitcoin and crypto evil.[41]

- Bill Gates remarked that due to their anonymity, cryptocurrencies have caused death.[42]

- Warren Buffett has urged investors to "stay away" from cryptocurrency (Bitcoin).[43]

- "The Wolf of Wall Street" Jordan Belfort has said there is no way world governments would allow a mass adopted cryptocurrency to survive.[44]

- "Mad Money" host Jim Cramer stated that Bitcoin was like "Monopoly money."[45]

The ironic part about most of these people is they are involved in crypto and blockchain in one major way or another. As you will see in an upcoming section, almost every major influential company is working in crypto and blockchain right now. Including JPMorgan, which is now quite invested in crypto, and is even rolling out its own token: JPMorgan Coin![46]

The cycle is almost like clockwork. As soon as the price of crypto starts to rise, a Wall Street talking head will talk about how it's a bubble and will ultimately go to $0.

Of course, the public demands answers from Wall Street and finance people when the subject of cryptocurrency comes up. Yet at the same time, systems and companies that these individuals have worked on and under their entire lives will be replaced by crypto. It's understandable that they would be biased.

As with any new technology, there will be evangelists and critics. It's a good debate that needs to be had in order to advance as a society. That being said, if we look to the past, we can see countless times when the experts were wrong—*specifically when the industry they made their name in was under attack:*

- **1889:** "Fooling around with alternating current (AC) is just a waste of time. Nobody will use it, ever."–Thomas Edison.[47]

- **1903:** "The horse is here to stay but the automobile is only a novelty–a fad."–President of the Michigan Savings Bank advising Henry Ford's lawyer, Horace Rackham, not to invest in the Ford Motor Company.[48]

- **1932:** "There is not the slightest indication that nuclear energy will ever be obtainable. It would mean that the atom would have to be shattered at will."–Albert Einstein.[49]

- **1981:** "No one will need more than 637KB of memory for a personal computer. 640KB ought to be enough for anybody."–Bill Gates, co-founder and chairman of Microsoft.[50]

- **2003:** "The subscription model of buying music is bankrupt. I think you could make available the Second Coming in a subscription model, and it might not be successful."–Steve Jobs, in Rolling Stone[51]

- **2007:** "There's no chance that the iPhone is going to get any significant market share."–Steve Ballmer, Microsoft CEO.[52]

Just because someone is an expert in one field, doesn't mean they know about crypto. This is why it's so important to learn about cryptocurrency for yourself.

Use experts to *advise* your course and give you new insights on both sides of the debate. And ultimately, take critics, especially talking heads, with an enormous grain of salt.

"Do As I Say, Not As I Do"

The world of finance is not "fair." If you or I want to get into investing, we open up a trading account with one of the big-name firms. We subscribe to the Wall Street Journal.

We keep our ear to the ground and hopefully have a network of people we trust to give us recommendations.

Not so with the big players like Goldman Sachs. With thousands of employees and billions of dollars at their disposal, these companies have armies of Ivy League analysts and sophisticated computer programs that can predict, as accurately as possible, where the market will move, and they have quicker ways to analyze and mitigate risk.

When they have the clear data that shows the market is *most likely* moving in a particular direction, they invest big.

With the big Bitcoin crash of 2018, millions of everyday investors exited the market, cashing out and deciding that Bitcoin was all hype, no substance.

Quietly, the billion-dollar multinational companies moved in to "buy the blood".

Why? Because they know the truth: Bitcoin opened Pandora's Box. Trustless, open and secure digital currency has not only been created, it's being used by millions of people, with billions of dollars in market cap. Many of these massive companies are seeing the writing on the wall. They can either choose to ignore it or profit from it.

Here is a short list of companies that service trillions of dollars in assets that have invested huge into cryptocurrency. Not in 2016. Not in 2017. But 2018...*after* the major crash.

Fidelity Investments

Fidelity Investments is the fifth-largest financial services company in the world, providing services for over $7.2 trillion in assets. In October of 2018, Fidelity announced its new crypto platform.[53]

It will now provide secure storage, a cryptocurrency trading platform, and investment advisory services.

SEC FinHub

On October 18, 2018, the SEC announced FinHub, "a resource for public engagement on the SEC's FinTech-related issues and initiatives, such as distributed ledger technology (including digital assets) [blockchain + crypto], automated investment advice, digital marketplace financing, and artificial intelligence/machine learning."[54]

Goldman Sachs

On September 6th, 2018, Goldman Sachs announced that its plans to develop a cryptocurrency for clients is well on its way and moving forward aggressively, as planned.[55] Goldman Sachs is also designing and will soon release a platform allowing its clients to trade cryptocurrencies.

New York Stock Exchange + Starbucks + Microsoft

In August of 2018, ICE, the owners of the famous New York Stock Exchange (NYSE), partnered with Starbucks and Microsoft to create a new crypto trading, custody, and payments platform called Bakkt.[56]

American Express

In May of 2018, American Express launched a blockchain that ties card purchases with rewards.[57]

Oracle

In July of 2018, Oracle announced a "Blockchain-as-a-service" company that will allow other companies to use the blockchain ledger without needing to develop their own technology in house.[58]

Tencent

In May of 2018, creators of "WeChat" TenCent partnered with the Chinese Government to explore blockchain solutions for tax fraud.[59]

Alibaba

The largest cross-borders e-commerce company in the world, Alibaba, has pledged to spend a significant portion of its recent $14 billion in funding on blockchain technology.[60]

Facebook

In December of 2018, Facebook announced it was hiring for its blockchain team. At the time of this writing, they are also working on their very first digital currency: Libra.[61]

TD Ameritrade

On October 3rd, 2018, TD Ameritrade announced its new crypto trading platform, ErisX. This new trading platform allows for both Bitcoin spot and futures trading.[62]

Amazon

Founded by the world's richest man, Jeff Bezos, this ecommerce megacompany offers cloud integration for multiple blockchains. They've also recently partnered with ConsenSys, "a global organism building the infrastructure, applications, and practices that enable a decentralized world."[63]

Nestle

Nestle is using blockchain to eliminate as many middlemen as possible throughout their entire global food empire.[64]

Pfizer

Pharmaceutical giant Pfizer is using blockchain to reduce costs in their supply chain.[65]

Anheuser-Busch InBev

In June of 2018, the creator of Budweiser announced their use of blockchain to simplify the logistics that come with transporting millions of cans of beer worldwide.[66]

Alphabet, Inc (Google)

As Bloomberg reports, "Google is working on blockchain-related technology to support its cloud business and head off competition from emerging startups that use the heavily-hyped technology to operate online in new ways."[67]

This is just a tiny sample of the companies currently investing in blockchain and crypto technology. What lessons can we learn from this? Blockchain and cryptocurrency are here to stay, and only growing bigger.

That's because decentralization isn't just powerful for individuals. It's a game-changer for massive companies.

Why? Because it'll allow these massive companies to both save and make billions of dollars, so these companies are investing heavily in the technology with no sign of stopping or slowing down.

World Governments

World governments have always been viewed as powerful enough to threaten cryptocurrency. With enough regulation, they could make it essentially illegal to trade with the coin. Anyone found trading the coin could be jailed for fraud, which would ultimately spell the end of the cryptocurrency revolution.

Or would it?

For starters, due to its nature, cryptocurrency is very difficult to take down. Crypto doesn't require a central hub or middle-man. Crypto is easy to transfer worldwide in seconds. And if you follow basic privacy protocol, it's almost impossible to trace you back to your crypto address.

Even in a worst-case dystopian future, where all the world governments block every crypto exchange by a firewall, this could be easily bypassed with a VPN.

Crypto is a peer-to-peer (p2p) technology. If the government was capable of shutting down p2p technology, then they would've already put a total stop to pirating media online. But it is technologically impossible.

Then there's the unmonitored, unregulated "dark web." Although few know how, it's actually very simple to gain access to and many illicit things are available there—on the internet. If the government could shut down a network like this, they would.

As I mentioned in the section on "consensus", cryptocurrencies require 51% of the entire network to make any significant change. With the sheer number of people involved in mining Bitcoin, co-opting this many machines and having them all agree to shut down the system would be nearly impossible.

The main way a government could regulate or fight against a cryptocurrency is by trying to make it difficult to cash out. They could ban banks from allowing you to turn cryptocurrency into cash.

However, they would have to do this worldwide, as otherwise, you could simply trade in your crypto for another country's currency. You could then change that currency back to USD (or whatever you like). Also, this is only effective if people *want* to cash out their cryptocurrency. As more and more avenues for spending crypto pop up, this type of ban could only be effective in the very short-term.

Another tried and true way to cash out your Bitcoin is OTC trading, also known as over-the-counter trading. At localBitcoins.com, they'll link you with people in your area who are buying or selling Bitcoin for cash. This way, you can meet someone who wants to buy or sell and go around any government roadblocks. This method is quite popular in China.

So, governments can *stall* crypto. They cannot prevent it. Now, let's take a look at how the various world governments have handled, and are handling, the "crypto problem":

China

In late 2017, China banned unregulated crypto exchanges throughout the country, claiming they represented a "financial risk." It also tightened regulation against miners, a huge chunk of which were operating inside China. This has caused many to leave to Europe and other areas where cryptocurrency is legal.[68]

China is largely considered the most powerful authoritarian regime in the world. Its attempts to brutally crack down on drugs, crime and government criticism have largely been effective within the country's borders. How about their crackdown on crypto?

Not so much. The South China Morning Post reported that "Chinese investors will always find ways to circumvent increasingly tightening controls over cryptocurrency trading by mainland authorities, making it practically impossible to ever impose a complete shutdown on trading."

Trading volume did fall after the government crackdown. However, the global crypto bear market followed shortly after, disincentivizing locals from finding and using workarounds. In the next boom, the crypto revolution will sweep over China as much as anywhere else.

However, recently China has started to warm up to blockchain and changed its regulatory policies. President Xi said in a speech on October 25, 2019 that he is endorsing investment in blockchain, saying that blockchain was a powerful technology that China needed to be a leader in.

Japan

We've seen Japan take an almost completely opposite approach to crypto as China took in its early days trying to regulate it out of existence. Although Japan initially declared Bitcoin was "not a currency"[69] in 2014, they reversed that statement in March of 2016, and crypto is now legal currency in Japan.[70]

India

In May of 2018, the Reserve Bank of India asked all banks in the country to free the accounts of cryptocurrency exchanges. They did not officially ban cryptocurrencies, but did what they could to make trading in them difficult. And in the fall of 2018, the Indian government announced they were looking into banning cryptocurrency altogether. This made trading cryptocurrency in India considerably more difficult.[71]

What happened? The volume of crypto trading actually increased by over 25%! Although the government did put barriers up, they were quickly bypassed by exchanges and traders.

Cryptocurrencies are built, from the ground up, to upset the traditional banking and monetary system that controls us all. They are far more flexible, durable and secure than the forces fighting against them. And honestly, it's not much of a competition. Just like a pistol always beats a sword, at some point in the upcoming future, *some* digital currency will win.

As of early 2019, India is still determining what to do with crypto. The current direction points to it being legalized, but highly regulated.

The United States

One of the most difficult tasks governments face with cryptocurrency is *defining* it. And there's no better place to watch this in action than in the United States.

In the USA, four separate government agencies have defined cryptocurrency in four unique ways:

1. **The Securities and Exchange Commission (SEC):** Defines cryptocurrency as a form of security, meaning people are buying and investing in crypto to generate a return. As such, every crypto exchange and trading platform must be registered with the SEC.[72]

2. **The Internal Revenue System (IRS):** Defines cryptocurrencies as a taxable form of property.[73]

3. **The U.S. Treasury:** Announced they would treat cryptocurrencies just like any other fiat currency.[74]

4. **Financial Crimes Enforcement Network (FinCEN):** Regulates cryptocurrencies as possible vehicles for money laundering and other financial crimes.[75]

It is overwhelmingly clear that crypto, as an entirely new asset class, can't be neatly sorted into previous definitions or regulations. By definition, a security can't be money. That means regulatory bodies within the U.S. government can't even agree on what crypto is! It is unlike anything they've ever grappled with before.

Each of these definitions remains fluid. For example, the SEC only recently announced that Bitcoin and Ethereum, the two largest cryptocurrencies on the planet, do *not* fall under the definition of "security."[76] Instead, the regulation is designed more to protect investors during ICOs.

These are the same people who are in charge of our social and financial lives! From LGBTQ rights to drug laws to cryptocurrencies, governments have demonstrated themselves to be slow moving, behind the curve, and generally incompetent time and time again. They are too busy trying to get re-elected, stay on "party lines", and gain personal influence to actually keep up with cutting-edge trends and technology.

Some Congressmen like Rep. Patrick McHenry (R., NC) and Warren Davidson (R., Ohio) do understand the nuances of crypto, and the societal shifts that are taking place. They are introducing meaningful bills and bringing thoughtful discussion into Washington, like the Financial Services Innovation Act.

If you would like to hear about the latest government crypto legislation… and learn how it could impact the market… visit crypto101insider.com

The Government Shutdown

In 2018, major news hit the cryptocurrency market: for the first time, the big money in finance would be able to buy and trade Bitcoin. This was supposed to be through the VanEck/Solid X Bitcoin ETF.

In the VanEck/Solid X ETF, one share would be worth 25 Bitcoins. Although this is far too expensive for everyday investors, it did allow the big money like major investment banks and top stock traders to start trading Bitcoin. This would inject a huge volume of cash into the crypto market, which many believed would end the bear market and lead to another crypto high.

Although this wasn't the first crypto ETF the SEC had seen proposed, it did address many of the issues the SEC had with other crypto ETFs they had reviewed. As a result, it had an extremely high chance of being approved.

Then disaster struck.

In early 2019, right when a decision by the SEC would be made, a disagreement between President Trump and the democrats forced a government shutdown. Suddenly the SEC workforce was operating at just 5%.

As a result, VanEck/SolidX pulled their ETF from review. Why? Because if the SEC *did* approve of their ETF, it's possible that the development would become headline news in the political battle.

Wasting no time, as soon as the government reopened, VanEcks resubmitted their proposal. But they also added in 40 pages of new content that they believed would make their proposal even more likely to be approved.

The SEC has 240 days to determine whether an ETF will be approved or denied. This has led many in the crypto space to groan, as the ETF was seen as a short-term savior for their crypto investments.

I recommend you look at it a different way. In a bear market, any bearish news will have a major downward impact on price...while any bullish news will have almost no impact.

Technical analysis is showing that crypto could begin a natural bull run very soon. If that's the case, how much better would it be for the ETF to come out around then? It would be like a shot of adrenaline to the bull market. Not only did the resubmission allow VanEck to make the proposal even better, it also delayed the announcement to a point in the future where it will probably have a much bigger impact.

This is why I keep reminding you to take the long-term view of crypto. If you are focused on the short-term, you will overreact. Small blips will make you panic or get overjoyed at every little thing that happens. Meanwhile, in the long-term, news that seems bad today could actually turn out to be great news tomorrow.

If you understand that the Crypto Revolution is inevitable, you can weather these hiccups. If you don't and you just want a quick win, you're not going to be able to survive long enough to really see the major gains.

When I first got into Bitcoin, I was a perfect example of what *not* to do. I was constantly refreshing the prices and reading all the news I possibly could. When the price would go up I'd stress about whether I should sell or not. When it dropped, I'd worry that my money was going to go to $0. It is human nature!

This is why I say that the people who made millions with Bitcoin *did not* have it easy. They had to weather all the news and the emotional ups and downs. I've heard endless stories about people who bought something with Bitcoin many years ago, and realize that if they didn't spend their bitcoin (on jeans, refrigerators, pizza, shoes…), they'd be millionaires!

You need to keep the future in mind and stay calm, cool, and collected—that is only possible when you know the long-term game. That's the difference between who I am now vs. who I was when I first invested. Now I know the game, I know where it's all going. And so I'm not worried at all about the ups and downs along the way. This is the approach I recommend you take as well.

Fake News Media

Thanks to the Internet, it's easier to learn information than ever before...on an exponential scale. It's also easier to *spread* information than ever before. Although the media has always preyed on humanity's most base impulses, with the rise of the Internet, the problem has gotten dramatically worse.

Now *anyone* can get online, write down their opinions, and publish them as news. If it contains the right emotional appeal, and pushes the right hot buttons at the right time, it can cause an overnight sensation.

Throughout the lifetime of Bitcoin, it has been featured constantly in the media. Now, although much of this may be designed to protect the financial systems and governments from the threat of crypto, much of it is a response to the mass market learning about crypto for the first time.

People have been skeptical of cryptocurrency and Bitcoin. For good reason–they haven't read this book. There are an enormous number of people who *want* to hear all the bad news they possibly can about cryptocurrency.

This is so they don't feel FOMO (fear of missing out). They didn't invest when Bitcoin was low, and so they hoped it would crash. The media played to this group of people and produced a massive amount of content speculating on Bitcoin and how it was most likely a fraud.

As the price of Bitcoin rose, the media fueled the fire by talking about the Bitcoin sensation. Talking about how people were mortgaging their homes and selling their cars just to invest more. When the price began to fall, the media caused a mass panic, leading to a major crash.

The truth is, people deserve to know what's happening in the crypto space. However, not having the right context hurts the movement in the short-term. I am not critiquing this movement or saying it shouldn't exist. I think the fact that it does exist is healthy human skepticism. That being said, it is a roadblock in the way of widespread crypto adoption.

Criminal Activity

Cryptocurrencies are built on a system of trustless data thanks to p2p consensus—what is, is. There is no subjectivity or extrapolation. Because the ledger is kept updated by the entire chain of users on the network, it is the most transparent system of money to ever exist.

Why, then, is it used by so many criminals?

The truth is, YOU— your name, address, DOB, SSN, etc. —are never shown in the blockchain. The only thing shown is your public address—a string of numbers that represent you, pseudonymously.

Now, if you access your crypto from your home computer, without taking any precautions, someone extremely technical with lots of research, and help from exchanges *could* trace your public address back to you. There are companies like Chainalysis that are working with crypto exchanges to do deep forensics on IP addresses and crypto transactions to link human identities to certain addresses. This is mainly for anti-money laundering and anti-terrorism efforts.

However, if you access crypto from an anonymous, secured connection, you will be able to make whatever transactions you'd like *with no link back to you.*

As a result, Bitcoin became popular on underground black markets like the Silk Road, where you could buy or sell anything anonymously.

Further compounding its usefulness to criminals is the fact that crypto is *easier to use.* You can send it worldwide in a matter of minutes. The fees are dramatically reduced. For all intents and purposes, it's *better money.*

Criminal enterprises are some of the least efficient businesses on the planet. They need to maximize any efficiencies they can get, and cryptocurrency provides one option for doing so.

Every single useful technology has been adopted and used by criminals. Simply put, bad people do bad things with technology. Good people do good things with technology. It will always be the case. Just because a handful of despicable criminals benefit from using cryptocurrency, doesn't mean we should withhold ourselves from all the benefits.

Let's not forget the billions of USD used by criminals every day to accomplish every illicit goal their twisted minds can come up with.

Technology is neither good nor bad. It's agnostic. It's human beings that use it for good or bad purposes.

14

The Million Dollar Cryptocurrency

As told by Bryce...

On July 17th, 2017, billionaire John McAfee, creator of the McAfee Anti-Virus (and a featured guest on the CRYPTO 101 Podcast), made a bold prediction. He predicted that by the year 2020, a single Bitcoin would be worth $1,000,000! [77]

He also stated that if it *didn't* reach that value, he'd eat his own genitals on live T.V…

Now, he made this prediction before the 2018 crash. And at this point, the price is not in-line to reach $1,000,000 by his predicted date.

That being said, I wanted to mention this seemingly outlandish prediction briefly, because it illustrates just how much potential *upside* there is in crypto investing. And many other prominent investors have made similar predictions in similar time frames.

Roughly 70% of the world owns a bank account or uses a mobile money provider.[78] Coinbase, the largest cryptocurrency exchange in the world (and the one you'll use to buy your first crypto in the next section), only has 20 million users.[79]

Many of these users will never buy more than $50 worth of crypto! In other words, the amount of people holding any real volume of crypto is tiny. To say cryptocurrency is in its infancy would be the understatement of the century. Crypto is still a fetus! Even though the price shot up with Bitcoin, and the hype was everywhere, it's just a *tiny* fraction of what's to ultimately come.

That's why at the beginning of this book, I was serious when I said crypto is the greatest wealth equalizer to ever exist. Even better, it's not only available to the rich, privileged and elite: it's open to you and I. Anyone with $1 can buy crypto. And as more and more people get involved, the price could skyrocket from there.

But enough of the theories and speculation. Let's get you involved!

15

How Investors Can Get Involved Before Crypto Mass Adoption

As told by Bryce...

Now, I'm going to teach you my VALUE formula for investing in coins from now into the future. That section is so important because this industry changes so fast. We wrote this book to be as timeless as possible in this space. That being said, it's not enough for me to tell you what I recommend now... *you need to be able to figure that out for yourself in the future.*

And that's what the VALUE formula is about. I'm then going to go over the top 5 new sectors of technology that are currently leaping forward. And I'm going to show you which cryptocurrencies, sometimes referred to as "altcoins" (i.e. *alt*ernative to Bitcoin) correspond with each new technology. That way you'll have at least 5 unique coins that fulfill the VALUE formula, in industries that are *most* *likely* to see astronomical, exponential growth in the next 10 years.

Lastly, you'll have a formula you can follow from now...until forever. Long after the information in this book is outdated, the VALUE formula will allow you to spot rising crypto opportunities...*long before they take off.*

Sound good?

I've made this point over and over again, and now I'll do it once more. The strategy I recommend in this book is a *long-term* one. However, always remember to do your own research before making any investment.

Later in this book, I will be walking you through the exact steps you need to pick up some crypto and join the movement yourself.

And, you might be ok just HODLing (holding) those assets and waiting for that moment to take your profits out of the market. During this time of holding, you'll hear talk like, "1 Bitcoin always equals 1 Bitcoin. I will never sell my coins! The person with the most Bitcoin will be king."

Basically, they're saying they will *never* cash out their crypto, because they're very confident that at some point,

Bitcoin will be THE currency, and it'll be much more valuable in the future than liquidating it for cash today.

I love these quotes to be honest. It's showing that the end game is changing the monetary landscape, using money that's more sound and worthy of our trust to build societies upon.

In the meantime, though...*there are plenty of ways to make profits with cryptocurrency right now.*

For the rest of the book, we will be discussing some advanced methods to do just that.

I am going to give you some examples of altcoins that are peaking my interest, and that are showing signs of considerable gain in the future.

But I want to make sure the book you are reading is timeless. I want to do more than just give you confidence in this book and my recommendations. *I want to give you confidence in yourself.*

So, I'll also be teaching you the exact formula I use personally to decide if a new coin is worth my investment. It's the formula I use, because it's the formula I was taught by some of the wealthiest and most successful investors on the planet. People who have made literally millions in cryptocurrency...and are still doubling down.

The VALUE formula isn't crazy technical. In fact, it's very simple. It is comprised of these simple steps:

1. **Evaluating Your Options**

2. **PROJECT vs BUSINESS**

3. **Identifying the Ideal BUY Point**

4. **Identifying the Ideal SELL Point**

Evaluating Your Options

Successful crypto investors don't try to reinvent the wheel, and I'm the same. Instead of creating my own methods, I've used the ideas and strategies from much better investors. If it's good enough for billionaires, it's good enough for me.

Despite his distaste for crypto, something he says he just doesn't understand, one of my favorite investors to draw inspiration and knowledge from is Warren Buffet. Buffet looks for companies he *understands* and keeps it very simple. Many have criticized him for avoiding tech companies and other industries, but by sticking to what he knows, he has been able to realize amazing returns.

Don't go buying some token in some industry you have no clue about. If people hear some hype about something and believe it's the next big thing, why do they go running to put money into it? FOMO! Plain and simple.

These people are quick to invest their money...and quick to lose it.

That's why, for starters, I recommend you keep your ear to the floor and specifically research which blockchain companies are in *your* industry. When you find a company that is working on something innovative *that you're an expert on*, you'll be able to understand blockchain in a deeper way. You'll also be able to feel out if it's ACTUALLY useful to the world.

To help figure this out, ask yourself, "what does the company do?"

For example, if you're a nurse, and a company is putting patient medical records on the blockchain, do you see a real use for that? How are they doing it? *Why* are they doing it? Is it a marginal or exponential leap in efficiency, privacy, security, etc.?

Ask yourself, "what is wrong with the current system and does this proposed solution actually make it better? Does it need blockchain?" If you say, nope they don't need blockchain to accomplish this task and it could be done cheaper and more efficiently, with greater security and ease *with a centralized database* (which is a huge possibility), then walk away.

If you want to learn about more projects and do a deeper dive into the tech and applications, check out our CRYPTO 101 Podcast episodes where we break everything down, piece by piece, with leaders in the industry. We have over 300 episodes!

Remember, although blockchain is revolutionary technology, it's also a buzzword. In the early days of the Internet, many investors made the mistake of believing *any* Internet company would be profitable...and lost billions of dollars as a result. Remember the original pets.com that had billions of dollars in "market value" upon listing during the Dotcom bubble that eventually went belly up? *Believe* that blockchain is powerful, but also have a healthy dose of *skepticism* with anyone claiming their blockchain application will change the world.

Now, if you determine that a company CAN actually benefit from blockchain, you understand the utility, and you can explain why it's using blockchain, we can move on to the next step.

PROJECT or BUSINESS?

Once you identify a company you think could be working on something really cool, I want you to dive deeper. A lot deeper. And the first way we're going to do that is put on our Sherlock Holmes hat and find out if we're looking at a project, or a business.

Due to the open source nature of blockchain technology, *anyone* can start a blockchain "project." That being said, the vast majority of these never make any money. They simply don't have the real-world use case to justify anyone actually spending money on whatever they're working on. Alternatively, what they're working on *could* have amazing value, but they lack the marketing and communication skills to tell the world about it.

I've seen and interviewed many businesses that have said all the right things such as, distributed social media, control and own your data, get paid for your content, etc. But, then you ask them, where does the money come from to pay me for my data or my content? They have no clue.

The best of them use a catch-all word like "advertisers." Then when you ask how many advertisers they have on their website, they say little to none. Then you ask the question, so how do *I* get paid? They say with our tokens. And the conversation repeats itself in a never-ending loop.

Look for a company that is generating revenue and is sustainable. Just by following this rule, you will eliminate the vast majority of bad blockchain investments out there. Understand where the demand for the token comes from, and how value flows back into the token.

Talk to the companies. In crypto, companies are making it very, very easy for you to talk to their teams. They're on social media. They tweet out updates. They welcome discussion. They're on Facebook and Telegram. Sometimes they have very comprehensive Slack or Discord channels where you can talk to their teams in a segmented way to know exactly what they're doing.

Take advantage of this openness and reach out. Don't be intimidated by the tech. Go to GITHUB or other platforms where they publish their code and verify that independent people have reviewed it--and made sure it's tested.

Then ask the developers about it. Let them walk you through it and explain it. Keep asking questions until you get it.

But wait! What about protocols like Ethereum, Cardano, and EOS? These could qualify as "projects", yet they are potentially extremely lucrative investment vehicles, too. What about companies that have a lot of money, but are currently in the building stage?

It's true that a protocol's "business plan" is to create a network and gain in value by people using it. But, think about it. Does Ethereum have a working product? Are people using it? Are teams developing applications on it? The answer is yes. So following the VALUE formula, you would know it's a smart investment.

Choose The Right BUY Point

"Every single bear market has turned into a bull, if you don't sell, you don't lose money."
-Tony Robbins.

Succeeding in crypto boils down to investing at the right time, and holding. So how do you know what the right time to invest is?

People try to time the market and get something a little lower, or try to sell it for a little higher. Look, there are traders on Wall Street that use the best software, have the fastest computers, and have Ivy League educations. And they all say the same thing: Don't try to time the market.

If you want to go in, invest. But you should be aware of the market. Just know if the macro trend you are in is a bull or a bear. As Warren Buffet says, "if you don't feel comfortable owning a stock for 10 years, you shouldn't own it for 10 minutes."

The reason you are putting money into a company or crypto is because you did your research. You know what they do, you know they have a plan, and you see their competitive advantage. So if you do not think that they will be worth more than you are buying in now at, then answer me one question…

Why are you buying?

Diversify. Now, I say this not meaning that you should put all of your money into all kinds of different companies. Look at compounding investments, interest, and indexes. Try to keep a portfolio of uncorrelated assets to manage risk.

The top coins, like the Fortune 500 companies, are top dogs for a reason. Because they are creating value now and into the future.

Would you like instant access to all of our crypto research, as well as follow our trades step-by step? Learn more at crypto101insider.com

Choose the Right Sell Point

So, we're in this for the long-run. Still, there will be ups and downs. And if we know what we're doing, these are the times we can profit the most.

When do you take your money out of the game? At the end of the day, this is about you and you alone. Everything so far in this book is to explain how *I* think. But it's not to tell you what to do. You should do what you feel comfortable with and make that decision with the most objective open mind as possible. The same goes for taking your money out.

Most traders will say you need to have a plan and stick with it. I agree with that theory, and yet I've fallen victim to FOMO and failed before.

Sometimes I forget to make plans in all the excitement. I never told myself that if I 3x my initial investment, I will pull out x amount of money. I never said I will take out my initial principal investment if I double it, and let the rest ride. There have been times where I just never said anything, and ignored logic. I promise you, all it takes is being burned once to promise yourself you won't be burned again.

Really take the time to think about what you want out of a particular investment. Make some hard rules for when you're going to sell. If the investment reaches that price...SELL. Don't rationalize your way out of it.

Times will be great and you'll think, "well even though my price target got hit, I'm going to hold on because it feels like it is going to go higher." This is a detrimental mindset. Plan your trade, and trade your plan!

Another issue people have is that they do not follow through with their plans. Let me ask you a couple questions, ok?

- Have you ever said, "I am going to lose weight" and never tried?

- Have you ever said, "I am going to go on a diet" and never changed your eating habits?

- Have you ever procrastinated on a project because...*insert excuse here*?

If you've said, "yes" to any of those, maybe you should not put money in. Why? Because you do not have the self-discipline to take your money out. Why do I say you need discipline?

Imagine this. You put in $500. You wake up one morning and you have $800. Two hours later you have $1,000. You go to sleep and wake up you have $1,200, and by the week's end you have $2,300. What did you tell yourself you were going to do? Did you tell yourself you'd take out your initial investment once it doubled? Did you?

If you didn't, why? Did you get caught up in the adrenaline of watching your money rise?

Don't be ashamed if you did. We have all done it. And you know what? We have all lost.

So in summary, what are some key ideas from this section?

1. Have a plan and stick to it

2. Think long-term

3.   Pull out initial investment so that the trade is "risk-free"

4.   Pull out profits on the way up

When it comes to the "Blue Chip" coins we discussed earlier, it's my opinion that it is best to hold these long-term. But when you're trading the more volatile and illiquid altcoins, when everyone is telling you to hold on for dear life, that may be the best time to sell. That's why you need to have a plan and stick to it.

Know that when you see big gains, you will have a crash. Don't worry about missing out on a little profit if you already profited. You cannot time or call the market. But you can take your profits. It is on you about how much risk you want to take on.

The Bottom Line

Rule #1: Don't lose money
Rule #2: Don't forget Rule #1

I told you how to evaluate a company, put money in, and take out your profits. At the end of the day this is all about one main goal: NOT LOSING MONEY.

Are you interested in investing and want to learn more about cryptocurrencies with the comfort of a community? Check out our content and community by going to: crypto101insider.com

16

ERC-20 Tokens

As told by Aaron...

As you dive deeper into the world of crypto, you'll hear the term "ERC-20" a lot. An ERC-20 token is a token designed to be used on the Ethereum network. These tokens follow a list of standards so they can be shared, exchanged for other tokens, or transferred into a crypto wallet. Examples of these types of tokens are Augur, Civic, & MakerDAO—just to name a few out of the hundreds of legitimate tokens.

*DISCLAIMER: The crypto market changes incredibly quickly. At the time of its publishing, these coins were market leaders. If you would like to know our **real-time** crypto recommendations, you can do so at crypto101insider.com*

To really explain ERC-20 tokens, we need to talk about Ethereum itself (which, if you follow the advice in this book, you'll be a proud owner of).

Taken from https://www.Ethereum.org/

Ethereum is a decentralized network of computers with two basic functions:

1.   A blockchain that can record transactions

2.   A virtual machine that can produce smart contracts

Because of these two functions, Ethereum is able to support decentralized applications (dApps). Think of it like the Apple App store with no sole owner! These dApps are built on the existing Ethereum blockchain, piggybacking off of its underlying technology. In return, Ethereum charges developers for the computing power in their network, which can only be paid in Ether.

So let's say a company wants to make a dApp or decentralized utility token. Instead of having to build an entire decentralized network from scratch, they can use Ethereum standards and design a token to work on their existing network. This saves time and money, and ensures a reliable network. These tokens, like any other cryptocurrency, can be traded on exchanges that list that specific token.

So now that you know what an ERC-20 is, how do you store them for safekeeping?

Using ERC-20 With Trust Wallet

Trust Wallet is a great mobile solution (iOS and Android) for keeping your ERC-20s, Bitcoin, or many other currencies on hand in a non-custodial fashion. In Chapter 24 we go through how to set up your Trust Wallet, but i'll briefly touch on it here. Remember your Ethereum address and your ERC-20 token addresses are the same.

On the homepage of your Trust Wallet, just press the looking glass on the top right and search for your token, put in its name, and add it to your list. Then simply tap the icon on your home page to see your receiving address. You can copy it by pressing the squares on the side of the address. Share this public address with anyone who needs to send you crypto, or use it to send crypto from one of your wallets to another.

Remember: If you're not sure if the token is an ERC-20 or not, just compare the addresses. Look at your Ethereum address and it should match the address for your ERC-20 token like MakerDAO or Augur. It will start with a "0x".

A Crash Course on Advanced Crypto Security

Crypto is still in the early days, which means it has a long way to catch up to existing financial technology.

If you're over 40, you remember life before ATMs. You'd have to take your bank book and ID, walk into a bank, and request to withdraw money. Usually you'd have to plan well in advance and know exactly how much you needed for the week so you didn't have to go back to the bank again. You'd keep that cash in your pocket, dishing out a bit here and a bit there, until you needed to go back to the bank and fill out forms.

Crypto is a lot like this at the moment. Taking proper security measures for your crypto involves storing it on a hard wallet. That way the majority of your crypto stays safe and out of the reach of hackers, while you can keep a small amount in your software wallet for spending purposes. Just like banking in the old days, when you want to transfer more crypto from your hardware to software wallet, you have to go through a process that can be inconvenient.

Remember...with crypto, **you own the bank. You ARE the bank**. As a result, the responsibility for getting your money to and from place to place falls solely on you. And, the responsibility for your crypto's *security* rests on your shoulders as well. Let's not forget, a vlogger with more than 100,000 followers got hacked for two million dollars due to poor security![80]

Proper security means developing new habits. Once these habits are formed though, not only will your crypto be safe, you'll have new security habits you can use in every aspect of your digital life. They will serve you well as we move further and faster into the future.

Because security is so important, I've peppered this book with best practices and reminders. At the risk of sounding repetitive, I am now dedicating an entire section of this book to the matter. That's because again, crypto takes personal responsibility. It's not something you just go out, buy, then the next day you're a millionaire.

Sure, that could become an *eventual* reality for you. In the meantime, you need to hold onto your crypto. And that involves keeping it safe.

I wanted to give you next-level security advice in this book.

The Lingo

OpSec, PerSec, InfoSec

OpSec

OpSec is short for operational security. It's a process that identifies critical information to determine if friendly actions can be observed by enemy intelligence. It then determines if this information could be interpreted as useful to them, and then executes selected measures to eliminate or reduce exploitation of friendly critical information.

In simpler terms, these are the practices, precautions and operations you take to preserve your digital security.

Loose Lips Sink Ships

The first digital security precaution you should take has nothing to do with technology. Summarized, it's simply this: keep your mouth shut.

You absolutely do not want to tell people about your crypto holdings. Think about it. If you just won the lottery, would you tell everyone you know? Would you drive around with a license plate that said Bitcoin? Would you tweet you've been holding Apple stock since the 80's, making you filthy, stinkin' rich?

I hope you wouldn't. *Because that makes you a target.* People see what you have and they want it. And if they can hack your entire digital life from the comfort of their own home, why wouldn't they? You never know who will overhear you. And, I hate to say something like this, but

you never know who your friends really are. Best not to test
your luck and keep your crypto secrets safe to yourself.

Passwords Management

Honestly, most people are password newbies. They don't
even change the factory password on their WiFi! They store
their private keys in Google docs. And maybe they even
use the same password for everything.

Are you guilty of any of these practices? If so, *you must
break these habits before entering the "Wild West" world of
crypto!*

I urge you to take my advice. Even if you don't *think* a
hack could happen to you, let me assure you: it can. I'd
rather you take my word for it now then wake up one day,
check your wallet, and see your account's been totally
drained.

Using "The Cloud" and Centralized Servers

Are you an iCloud user? What about Dropbox or Google
Drive? These are great apps that make our lives easier. *But
they can also be hacked.* And if you have your crypto
private keys or recovery phrases on these servers, your
money is as good as gone.

When a hack like this happens, it doesn't generally make the news. It's treated as a "small" breach. Yet in that "small" breach, maybe 1,000,000 accounts were compromised! And you wouldn't even know it. You wouldn't hear about it on the news. And usually, it's the fault of the company you're storing it with. Someone got lazy, made a mistake, or cut corners. It happens. Often.

For example, the massive Yahoo hack in 2014 exposed half a billion users! This hack was possible because Yahoo was using a hashing algorithm that was known to be prone to collisions.[81] Let me break down what that means, because it has huge implications for crypto.

Hashing Algorithm

A hashing algorithm is defined as follows:

"A mathematical algorithm that maps data of arbitrary size to a hash of a fixed size. It's designed to be a one-way function, infeasible to invert.[82]"

Hashing takes a simple input and turns it into a complicated, impossible to guess string of letters and numbers. Currently there are many of these hashing algorithms in use for the cryptocurrency space. Bitcoin uses Secure Hash Algorithm (SHA)-256, rightfully named because it produces a 256-bit output hash. Other hashing algorithms include Script, Equihash, SHA-1, SHA-3, and cryptonight. (A complete list of algorithms with their crypto asset can be found at whattomine.com.) Let's talk about how a hash works:

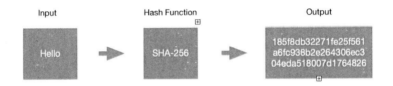

Using the input of "Hello World" from figure 1, the input is run through a hashing function and a hash output is received. A SHA-256 input produces a 256 bit or 32 byte output (Schneier, 2005). There are a couple rules that a hash algorithm needs to follow.

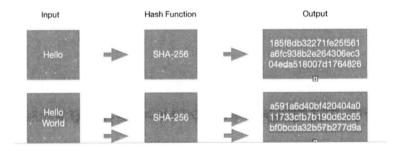

1. It must be computationally easy to take your input hash and make an output.

2. It must be computationally infeasible to take a hash and extrapolate the input from the output hash.

Please note that this is infeasible but not impossible. As of right now the number of computations it would take to extrapolate an input from an SHA-256 hashing algorithm is 2^{256} or 1.157×10^{77}.

3. It must be deterministic. This means that the same input will always have the same output.

4. Slight changes in messages make a totally different hash. For example, we've already determined the hash output of Hello. But what if we add a space after Hello? As you can see, the hash output totally changed. Now what if we changed Hello to Hello World? The hash output changes again. (More on this in a bit)

5. It must be infeasible for two messages to produce the same hash. Again, this is an infeasibility, not an impossibility. There is always a possibility for two different inputs to produce the same output. If this ever happens, it's called a collision.

    1. Even though the odds against a collision are absolutely massive (2^{256} to 1), that is still a finite number.

2. There are different attacks that hackers can carry out

    1. Collision: "A collision attack occurs when it is possible to find two different messages that hash to the same value." (Morton & Smith, 2014)

    2. Preimage: "a preimage attack on cryptographic hash functions tries to find a message that has a specific hash value." (Morton & Smith, 2014)

PerSec

This is divulging personal information about yourself that could be used to hack you.

For example, let's say you get into a conversation with a complete stranger. They get you to divulging your hometown, name of your first pet, your mother's maiden name, your high school, etc. This information could be used to build a profile on you in order to reset passwords and steal your digital information.

Think about the difference between OpSec and PerSec this way. Good OpSec would simply be avoiding a conversation with a stranger. That way, you'd never be put in a situation where you divulge this information. Good PerSec, on the other hand, is going into a conversation with a stranger *aware*, so you know NOT to divulge any of this information, no matter how clever they may be.

Please do not think that when I say "stranger", I only mean someone you meet in real life. We live in a digital world, and this stranger could very easily be the operator on a phone, a private message on Facebook or Instagram (posing as a high school friend), or it could be a beautiful member of the opposite sex that takes an interest in you seemingly at random.

InfoSec

InfoSec is just an umbrella term used to mean protecting information. This information could be your passwords (where you store them), your private keys, and potentially even your public keys.

Why protect your main public keys? Because Ethereum, Bitcoin, and many other blockchains are transparent. They have an open ledger. With your public key, someone could possibly trace transactions back to you, exposing your crypto holdings.

You should always practice SAFE SECs! (wink wink). When you practice safe secs, you have good (cyber) hygiene. This also is a warning that you shouldn't blindly trust websites to have your best interest in mind.

So now you know the terms.

Putting It Into Action

Now I want to tell you about multi-factor authentication (MFA), and two-factor authentication.

MFA is an authentication method where the computer user is granted access only after they successfully present two or more pieces of evidence that they are who they say they are. This kind of evidence comes in three forms:

1. Knowledge (something the user and only the user knows)

2. Possession (something the user and only the user owns)

3. Inherence (something the user and only the user is)

Multifactor Authentication is the ultimate in digital security, which is why it's used by all the best crypto exchanges. Take Coinbase, for example. If you haven't logged in for a while, you will need to go through your normal 2FA process, but you'll also need to confirm a code sent to your email. This process is only needed if you haven't logged in for a while, or you're accessing your account from new WiFi or different geographical locations.

Two-factor authentication (also known as 2FA) is a type, or subset, of multi-factor authentication. It's a method of confirming a user's claimed identity by using any combination of these different factors: 1) something they know, 2) something they have, or 3) something they are.

If you are using sites now that do not have 2FA, then I would suggest that you stop using those sites, or at the very least, make sure they're not vital and you're not storing personal information there. If you have sites that do use 2FA, please make sure it's enabled and you're using one of these apps:

Storing Your Crypto Security Assets

Key ● = Supported X = Unsupported	Google Authenticator	Authy	Yubico	DUO	FreeOTP	Authenticator Plus	SoundLogin
Fido (U2F)	●	●	●	●	●	●	**N/A**
Multiple Token	●	●	●	●	●	●	●
Smart Phones	●	●	X	●	●	●	●
Desktops	X	●	●	●	X	X	X
Open Source	X	●	X	●	●	X	X
Multiple Device Syncing	●	●	X	●	X	●	X
Offline Mode	●	●	●	●	●	●	●
RDM Integration	●	X	●	●	X	X	X

Becoming a fully-fledged crypto citizen requires you to take responsibility for a number of crypto security assets. You may have hardware wallets, private keys, written passwords, YubiKeys, and more. So how can you safely store them? There are a few options.

One, you could keep your hardware wallet and printouts at your house, in a fire-resistant safe, with your docs in a fire-resistant bag. Make sure your safe is secured to the floor. (I recommend a basement with cement screws anchoring it down.) If you don't trust it at your home or you move often, get a safety deposit box at your bank.

Now, let's talk about a security issue you probably haven't thought of yet: what if you die?

As of the writing of this book, there are no laws about cryptocurrency inheritance. And even if there was, if your family members or loved ones don't have your private keys and you pass away, no government or law enforcement agency on the planet could help them recover them.

I recommend writing a handwritten letter to your family or loved ones and putting it into the safe or lock box. In this letter, let them know what cryptocurrency is, why you have it, how to check its worth, and how to access it, move it and cash it out.

To give them access to the safe, you can have a lock box in the bank with the safe code. Or you can have the code in your last will and testament.

We keep a constant watch for new crypto scams. As soon as we find one, we alert our community about it, and give them detailed instructions on how to avoid it. Learn more at crypto101insider.com

17

Crypto's Hottest Industries

As told by Bryce...

So far, we've talked big picture crypto—how it's going to change the world, and how it already has. Now for the fun part: the future.

Two of the most powerful companies on the planet are Amazon and Google. 25 years ago, neither of them existed. Thanks to the power of the Internet, these companies now have more control than most governments. In just 25 years!

I'm telling you this to illustrate how quickly new technology can change the world. 50 years ago, it would've been virtually impossible to imagine life today. We're living in the future!

The following are the projects that make me excited and passionate about the future of this space.

Industry #1: Exchanges

Exchanges are the doorways to crypto. Kucoin (KCS), Binance (BNB), and Bitfinex (LEO) are examples of an exchange platform that each have their own token. The token's value is a function of how much volume is traded on the exchange and how much profit is generated by the exchange. Just like going to the bank to get money, you need exchanges to get crypto, and owning a piece of an exchange like this through their token can provide much needed diversification to your crypto portfolio. Exchanges are one of the financial foundations for cryptocurrency. The better the exchanges are, the more access people will have to crypto.

So where are we at with exchanges right now? There are three types of exchanges:

1. Centralized

2. Decentralized

3. Hybrid

The three aforementioned exchanges are all centralized. This is a large company that allows you to purchase and store crypto on their platform. However, they also control everything that goes on within that platform. This is why we say that until you own your keys with your crypto stored on a wallet, you don't own your crypto—the exchange does.

A centralized exchange is, currently, the easiest way to get involved in the space. Because a centralized exchange is owned by one main party, they can create a seamless user experience, allowing you to easily exchange your fiat currency for crypto, and then exchange that crypto for other coins.

Yet to some extent, these centralized exchanges ironically go against the founding principles of cryptocurrency, mainly, decentralization.

That can lead to problems.

For example, in 2016, a man named Craig Wright gained a lot of notoriety in the crypto space. Why? He claimed to be Satoshi Nakamoto, the original anonymous inventor of Bitcoin. And, he claimed to have proof.

He also released his own coin, Bitcoin SV. This, he said, held true to his "original vision" for Bitcoin, which had now been sabotaged by the hard fork that created the altcoin Bitcoin Cash.

However, many in the crypto space doubted his proof, and did what they could to debunk it. As a result, centralized exchanges like Binance refused to allow BSV to be bought on their platform.

This is an example of what a centralized exchange does: control the platform.

Whether or not you think Craig Wright is Satoshi, or if he's a scammer, it doesn't change the point—centralized exchanges, at any point, can dictate WHO is allowed to be hosted on the exchange. As long as you have one centralized player with control over an entire platform, that is a move towards centralization, like Fiat, and away from decentralization, the core founding principal of the crypto movement.

There's another problem with centralized exchanges: hacks.

Although today's centralized exchanges take absolutely massive security precautions and are considered quite safe, they do carry the danger of being hacked and there are always risks involved.

We've seen this in the past with exchanges like Mt. Gox being hacked and losing hundreds of millions of dollars worth of crypto.[83] Again, it's another reason why I highly, highly, highly recommend you DO NOT store your crypto on a centralized exchange. Although centralized exchanges are difficult to hack, hackers do have major incentives to try because if they succeed, they gain access to an absolutely enormous amount of money.

On the other hand, you have decentralized exchanges, or DEX.

Decentralized exchanges are on the blockchain, which means for all intents and purposes, they're impossible to hack. They also do not have any central ruling figure and allow any coin to be exchanged on the network.

The problem with a DEX though is they aren't very user friendly. Specifically, there is no "onboarding" method to exchange your fiat currency into crypto. If you want to use a DEX, you must already have crypto to begin with (that you bought through a centralized exchange).

This is why I believe DEX platforms are one of the most exciting growing spaces in the crypto industry. As soon as someone figures out a method for decentralized onboarding, that exchange will naturally become the "go-to" over other centralized providers. It's only a matter of time.

The hybrid exchange, where certain decentralized features are used in a centralized platform, hold great promise. Though not as well-known as centralized and decentralized exchanges, hybrids could become much more popular over time and change the way we buy and sell crypto.

With this knowledge of how exchanges work, you can also look to the Fortune 500 companies that are creating their own exchanges to see potential opportunities to invest. For example, Facebook is working on developing a stable coin called Libra.

When it launches, you will likely be able to use your credit card on Facebook to buy the coin, and use it as a payment method on other partnering platforms, like Uber, Lyft, and many more. Once you have that coin, you own crypto, and can then use a DEX. So by creating its own coin, Facebook itself becomes a method for onboarding.

Questions to ask yourself when looking into this sector:

- How are they making it easier for people to onboard?

- Can my mother figure this stuff out?

- Are they insured?

- Can regulatory bodies shut them down?

Let's break it down.

How are they making it easier for people to onboard?

This is an important one. Because even though crypto is getting easier and easier to get into, it can still be confusing. It requires a radical shift in mindset and responsibility. Essentially, unplugging from the "system", and plugging into a world where YOU are the system.

You have to learn about private and public keys. Long strings of numbers and letters as an "address" that you need to be very careful with.

Some blockchains still have slow transfer times. Anti-criminal regulation has created hurdles. These are all barriers to entry that make it difficult for everyday people to get into cryptocurrency.

Companies like Coinbase are making it easier and easier. In fact, just the other day I helped a friend sign up for Coinbase during her lunch break. She was done in 15 minutes. Throughout the process, she kept asking me how secure it all was.

It's nerve-racking for people to give their personal data to a company. This will become so much easier with identity on the blockchain. And that's just one area where the industry is likely to see massive growth.

Can my mother figure this stuff out?

Exchanges like Coinbase are easy enough for anyone to figure out. Once you venture off the platform though, it gets a lot more complicated. Especially when you start to invest in other altcoins and projects. One glance from a novice at a fancy exchange with hundreds of cryptocurrencies, order books, charts, and price quotes will have them running in fear.

Another problem is transferring crypto. It's easy to sign up, it's easy to connect your bank, but transferring is still way too complicated and scary.

Are they insured?

This is an important question for a couple different reasons. The first is the protection of your fiat or crypto. The second is that if they're insured, you know that an insurance company has looked at their operations under a microscope. They've made sure the exchange is using the absolute best practices. An insurance company wants to collect the premium—not pay out. And they will only work with an exchange where that is their most likely reality.

Can regulatory bodies shut them down?

As of the writing of this book, crypto is in a safe place. It's been threatened from all angles, by governments and other forces, but has weathered them all. That being said, we're still in such early days. What happens when it really starts making waves?

What happens if there's an economic catastrophe and investment banks start hedging into Bitcoin and other cryptoassets instead of gold, bonds, or dollars? The government won't like that. How can they stop it? One way they might try is to do what China tried in 2017—stop the means of trading and purchasing crypto.

As we've discussed, no matter how much a government may want to shut down cryptocurrency, it's virtually unstoppable. Why? Decentralization and cryptography. They can't compromise EVERY node.

Now, wouldn't it be amazing if we used those two qualities to make an exchange that could never be shut down?

Well, it's already happened with decentralized exchanges, which make it very tough for governments to stop the flow of cryptocurrency, peer-to-peer.

Industry #2: Payments

On June 29, 2007, Steve Jobs announced the first ever iPhone. When it launched, Microsoft CEO Steve Ballmer was quoted saying, "There's no chance that the iPhone is going to get any significant market share."

As we look back, we know just how wrong he was. The iPhone changed absolutely everything, and smartphones are now an integral part of our day-to-day lives.

So, was his opinion uneducated and ignorant? I'd argue it wasn't. Let me explain:

Ballmer, like most of us, was using what he knew to be true in order to make an informed decision. I remember when the first iPhone came out.

I remember looking at the Palm Pilots and Blackberries (brands that went the way of the Dodo) thinking their screens would make for a horrible user experience. Up until the iPhone, touch screens were slow, pixelated, unresponsive, and seemed to have layers upon layers of plastic over them.

So, when Steve made that comment, it was easy to see where he was coming from. Nothing at that point was good enough to do away with all the buttons. Tactile buttons worked! They were fast and we were all used to them!

However, once we all got our hands on the iPhone, our opinions started to change.

Why?

Look. The first iPhone, just like Bitcoin, was not perfect in its first rendition. If you recall, the first iOS didn't even have copy paste. But Apple improved it with updates. And, third-party apps made the iPhone experience better and better.

It wasn't until someone used an iPhone for the first time that they truly understood the utility. It wasn't until they had a camera, iPod, phone, texting, Internet, YouTube and social media in a single device in their pocket, that it all clicked.

I would actually go a step further. Even after using the iPhone, most didn't understand its full potential. But, they knew instantly that they could not and would not ever live without it again.

This is cryptocurrency.

Some of the loudest critics of crypto are people who point to different systems they use now and show how they are totally capable of doing what we need them to do—that crypto is unneeded and obsolete.

For example, Apple Pay, credit cards, debit cards, PayPal, Venmo, etc. These are all quick and reliable ways to make everyday purchases. You rarely have a problem or a delay with your purchase. So, for the people using these methods of payments daily for their daily lives, cryptocurrency is not a solution.

That is, until you really start using it.

Then, just like the iPhone, you realize the massive impact cryptocurrency has on payments. Transacting all your daily needs can be done on a cryptocurrency, true. But it also does so much more!

With cryptocurrency, you'll never have to explain to a bank or other gatekeeper who you are sending money to and why. You'll never be blocked by your credit card when making overseas transactions. You'll never be embarrassed in line when your card is declined because the purchase looks suspicious. You'll never be charged 3% overseas transaction fees. You'll never be charged $5 to withdraw from an ATM.

Because your money is where you are when you need it: In the global blockchain that you, and only you, can access at any time. It moves with you AT THE SPEED OF LIFE.

Drawn out to its logical conclusion, Bitcoin can be the debt settlement layer for all banks worldwide.

Bitcoin may not be the perfect currency. Just like the iPhone, at release, wasn't the perfect phone (and still isn't to this day).

But, what Bitcoin gave us is proof of product. Beyond that it showed real market demand as evidenced by the extreme rise in price. Bitcoin showed us all that this was something the people of the world wanted and needed. Just like the iPhone, it created a system that was exponentially better than multiple entire industries combined.

The future is going to be far faster than anything we experience today, which will require you to be your own bank and transact anywhere in the world at a moment's notice. Without restrictions, without regulations, without banks, and without intermediaries.

This future is being built out of necessity. It's being built out of gross manipulation of our data by irresponsible companies. It's being built out of the ashes of the insane greed massive banks demonstrated during the 2008 financial crisis. It's being built out of horrible practices and fiscal irresponsibility in other countries and at home.

The power of Bitcoin payments can only be understood by possessing and using it. Then you will understand.

Industry #3: Internet of Things

Let me paint a picture for you.

One day in the not-so-distant future, you'll wake up to the smell of fresh coffee. Your coffee maker will have already prepared you a cup, exactly how you like it, and poured the exact proportions of coffee and water to get your fix. You'll walk downstairs and the lights will turn on automatically, your A/C will adjust to your preferred temperature, and your TV will turn on to your usual news channel.

Your self-driving Uber meets you outside, since it knows you want to be picked up from your house at 8:30am. On the dot. It knows that you were listening to BBC World News just a minute ago, so it has it on when you enter. It picks the most efficient route, and knows in advance where there's an empty parking spot to let you out at. Your mornings, and every other minute of your day, will be powered by data. Your data.

The Internet of Things (IoT) movement will birth multi-billion and maybe even multi-trillion dollar companies. All developed on your data. That doesn't seem fair, does it?

But what if there was some way you could monetize your data? Charge the companies a fee for the data you generate all day? From your online purchases to your TV viewing. From podcasts to what's in your refrigerator and how much you eat. What if all of that data was somehow owned and controlled by you?

Once again, blockchain makes this happen. There are companies using blockchain to make a private key for your data, giving you the control. The writing is on the wall. We know this is coming. You can't even load a webpage anymore without dozens of targeted ads screaming at you.

Marcus East, the former CTO of National Geographic who is currently working at Google in the office of the CTO, came on the CRYPTO 101 Podcast recently. He believes access to data is a human right, and that the more data we have, the better decisions we can make. I couldn't agree more. But, where is that data? Who has it? How can we access it?

Pay attention to companies making oracles that connect all of this data being generated by you together.

IoT is going to connect people in indescribable ways. Complex AI algorithms will be able to connect seemingly random bits of data from the weather conditions, amount you slept, what you ate yesterday, and how much you walked, to generate an incredibly accurate health snapshot. Diseases like cancer may be predicted by IoT devices comparing your data to data of those with the disease.

Again, where will these companies get this data? *From you.*

This kind of data is something we all generate for free already, every single day. The companies that figure out this solution will allow us to get paid for simply being ourselves.

Finally, IoT and blockchain provide solutions to some enormous problems looming on the horizon. Driverless cars and trucks will displace millions from their jobs. How are these people supposed to get paid?

A possible solution is that they'll own the trucks. With smart contracts (remember to visit CRYPTO 101 episodes about smart contracts) and blockchain tech, it's possible for people to have small stakes in the trucks that are driving around.

Imagine this: you have $10,000. That's clearly not enough to buy your own self-driving big rig. But, it is enough to buy 7% of one.

A quick google search shows that an independent truck driver can earn gross revenue of around $180,000 a year. 70% of that is cost. Thus, an independent truck driver can net around $54,000 a year. But that's a human driver!

Let's kick that up a bit. The self-driving truck will not need to sleep or eat. The truck can now also drive at higher speeds for longer periods. So, let's put revenue at $250,000. Let's also assume that 70% is cost (which I think is high) and 30% is profit. That leaves $75,000 to be divided up between the truck owners. Your 7% now gets you $5,200 a year income. In two years, you've made back your initial investment. And you profit every year thereafter.

Maybe you decide to take all of the profits and put them back into buying more shares in driverless trucks. Now, in only 10 years you own 2.56 trucks with an income of $192,000 a year. All of this is possible by smart contracts, blockchain tech, and micro payments.

Highly specialized blockchains like IOTA are working to make all this a complete reality—autonomous, machine-to-machine value transfer. They've got partnerships with companies like Jaguar and Bosch to give digital wallets to cars and other machines. Other IoT applications are being built on top of more generalized smart contract platforms like Ethereum, EOS, and NEO.

Industry #4: Privacy

One of the biggest reasons why Bitcoin and the distributed ledger caught on is transparency. Most people like the idea of the public being able to audit banks, companies, politicians, governments and charities at will.

The common thought is that with this transparency, there will be less fraud, exorbitant salaries, irresponsible government spending, money laundering, and any other violations you can think of. I would agree with this. However, when it comes to the individual—to you and I— that's where transparency breaks down.

We don't *want* the world to be able to look at us under a microscope without our consent.

The naive argument I usually hear is, "well if you're not doing anything illegal, then you have nothing to worry about", which is an absolutely stupid statement. Why? Because there are many completely legitimate reasons for someone to want to keep certain completely legal transactions private.

Bitcoin gave us a vision of the future. It gave us a product that we needed. A currency that can grow with us into the future of this global, interconnected community. We do not need Visa, fiat, or PayPal now. We need money that can cross borders instantly when we want it to. We need to send payments where we want and to whom we want.

Why? Because this is the new world. We have the capability to unlock "value" and let it flow freely between a global village, but government constructions have disabled the free flow of value—it is hurting our chances to become stronger and better as a species. It's a world where we have friends and relationships everywhere, all over the globe.

Be it business, friendship, or a 6 degrees to Kevin Bacon relationship—we are globally connected at the speed of light, or as I like to say AT THE SPEED OF LIFE. That's the future I'm trying to get across to you in this book. The future is fast. And we'll expect our money to be the same.

Bitcoin gave us that. It proved that not only can we be our own bank, not only do we *not* need overseers to decide how we can use our hard-earned money, it facilitated a new kind of global relationship.

Until it didn't.

Imagine this. Your nan (British for grandma) has cancer. The doctor has her on pain medications and other chemical concoctions for nausea. You and your family are thinking that she'd love to try CBD or cannabidiol oil instead. You've heard that it's not only more effective, but non-addictive. There's just one problem:

It's illegal.

You find a website that can get you CBD oil, but they only take Bitcoin. Since CBD is illegal in your country, if you pay with card or bank transfer, the bank would report it to the authorities, and you could go to jail. Or, at the very least, you wouldn't be able to get the medicine to make your nan more comfortable.

Bitcoin was thought of as the end-all solution to this situation. Until it wasn't. With the transparency of the Bitcoin blockchain you can still see every transaction. With deep blockchain forensic analysis as made possible by companies like Chainalysis, if someone uses the same wallet or address repeatedly, it's possible to figure out who actually controls the wallet. If that happens, the person buying CBD could be caught for buying an illegal substance.

So does this mean privacy is only useful when buying illegal substances?

There are many reasons why you'd want your privacy. Imagine your employer discovers you're purchasing a certain medication. Would they perceive you and/or your work differently? What if you were buying adult toys on Amazon? Would you want your friends to know what you and your partner do in the bedroom? Or, do you want your coworkers to know how much money you have in the bank? What about your political donations?

Privacy is fundamental and vital for individual freedom. Which is why there's been an evolution to Bitcoin's open ledger: privacy coins.

A privacy coin is a cryptocurrency that hides data about its users. At minimum, privacy coins hide identities. They also often hide the amount of cryptocurrency traded and held in wallets.

Bitcoin is not a true privacy coin. Bitcoin users are identified by their public address. Bitcoin transactions and wallets are publicly visible data by their very nature.

This is an important step for cryptocurrency, because you can do everything you could with Bitcoin, without potentially sacrificing your privacy.

Zcash, Dash, and Monero are the three most popular privacy coin options. One other option is MimbleWimble, and the coins that use MimbleWimble: Grin and Beam.

MimbleWimble is a blockchain format and protocol that provides extremely good scalability, privacy and fungibility by relying on strong cryptographic primitives. It addresses gaps existing in almost all current blockchain implementations.

Industry #5: Identity

Centralized companies control all of your data. I'm not just talking about Facebook and Google. I'm talking about companies you may have never heard of like Equifax. Most people didn't even know they existed until a data breach exposed the private information of 146 million people to the world.[84]

Think about that for a minute. There was a company that held all of the information used to determine your credit score, that you might not have even known existed until it was too late!

There are people right now with bad credit not able to finance homes or cars. We blindly TRUST a system, a company, to have the correct information. We count on that score to go to banks to get loans to secure housing for ourselves and our families. And the company that controls your data and is making the decisions gets hacked. Which begs the question: How do you know your score is really your score? How do you know it wasn't tampered with?

You can't audit Equifax. You don't have any say in what the rules are governing your credit score. Yet we, as an entire society, trust them.

Another scary misuse of data came recently with Cambridge Analytica. Again, a company no one knew existed until the consequences were too big to ignore. I want to emphasize too big to ignore. If only 1 million people lost their data with Equifax, it probably would've been swept under the carpet. This is happening all the time.

Cambridge Analytica showed our data being used to sway an election. Not hack a computer, but basically hack the minds of people through social media.[85] It was a way to see our likes and dislikes, and our fears and desires. They then designed a campaign to use what they learned about you to manipulate you.

None of this is conspiracy, it is fact. Governments and companies grab your data and use it against you. And, if you want to use Facebook and other social media sites as a way to connect with friends or family, this is something you are forced to put up with.

Ancient wisdom advises us to think for ourselves. But how can we when there are teams of Ivy League PhDs designing AI many times smarter than humans to learn about you, and push your buttons in just the right way?

Well, blockchain, again, may hold the answer.

Let's think of all the ways you have identity right now:

- Your driving record

- Your credit information

- Your criminal record

- Your voting record

- Your banking records

- Your medical records

- Your dental records

- Your travel records

Everything that makes you, *YOU*, all in the control of bloated bureaucracies. Most of this data you can't even access. In fact, my close friend once had to drive from one state to another just to pick up medical records for his wife. All because the two hospitals didn't use the same medical records system and couldn't (or wouldn't) transfer the information for the other hospital to use.

This is real!

Now, imagine that when you're born, you're given a private key. That private key is encoded to your biometrics. Your face ID + fingerprint + pin code allows you to access these records. And they're all stored on a blockchain.

Imagine that wherever you are you have the information you need. And, others can gain access to it too (with your permission).

Imagine going to the doctor on vacation and using your face ID, fingerprint and digital pin to unlock your WHOLE LIFE'S medical data for the doctor?

Imagine the same checks being used for you to vote online. Or, when going to the bar and proving your age. Or, applying for a job and proving your education and your criminal record.

How does all this information get into the blockchain? Well, all of these different institutions have PUBLIC keys to your personal blockchain. Just like an old blue mailbox on the corner, where people can put mail into it and only the mailman can take it out, the information of your life can be the same way.

Your information goes wherever you go. And the only people who can access it are the people you give permission to. That is living at the speed of life!

Industry #6: Financial Services

REMEMBER: In 2018, US banks raked in $237 billion dollars in profit. That's *profit.* Which means it's how much they made *after* the enormous, bloated executive salaries. The bonuses. The private jets. The 5-star hotels. The expensive meals. The global conferences. After all of it, they made $237 billion in pure profit!

How do they do it? With your money! As we've discussed, Fractional Reserve Banking allows them to keep roughly 10% of your money in the bank, and loan the other roughly 90% out to anything they want.

They buy stocks. The buy bonds. They sell mortgages. And what do you get for allowing them to invest your money? According to the FDIC the average annual interest rate for savings accounts is 0.09%.[86]

Could this be different? What if you had total control of your money? If someone wanted to use your money for investments, loans, and mortgages, what if they had to make it beneficial not only to them, but also to you? And if you did end up letting them use your money, you gave it to them in a smart contract with a guaranteed promise of a good return? Wouldn't that be nice?

This is one possibility with cryptocurrency. Because with cryptocurrency, you own and control your money with your private keys.

When you give your money to the bank, they are in control of your money. They're the custodians of your money. There have been instances in history where banks either didn't want to or couldn't give clients their money back.

Why? Because, at the end of the day, the money stored in the bank became the bank's. With crypto, it's different. You would control and own your money. If you did give it to a third-party to loan it out or make use of, it would be locked in a smart contract. With this system you just have to trust the code, not people, institutions, or governments. It's trustless.

One extremely impressive project built on top of Ethereum is called Maker and they are building a decentralized bank.

Maker is a DAO (decentralized autonomous organization) comprised of a decentralized stablecoin, collateral loans, and community governance. Their resilient stablecoin Dai is an asset-backed, hard currency for the 21st century. It is designed to maintain a stable $1.00 value and has the same benefits of other cryptos—no borders and no restrictions.

Users of Maker can gain additional liquidity from their crypto assets so that you can lend yourself a secure and stable form of money. Users can also open a collateralized debt position (CDP) to increase their exposure to an underlying asset and effectively trade on margin.

Lastly, with the most radical and innovative aspect of Maker, anybody can gain influence over the decisions impacting the system through ownership of the MKR token. MKR is the governance token for the Dai Credit System. MKR holders have the important responsibility of making decisions around risk that will impact the future of the system. MKR holders get the privilege of voting on stability fees, interest rates, debt ceilings and more. Would your bank ever let you vote on such things?

Banking for the Unbanked

The unbanked is a collective term for people who cannot use banking services and therefore, have little or no access to financial services.

There are many reasons why a person may be unbanked, including:

- The infrastructure and trust does not exist in their country.

- After experiencing a banking crisis, they may have a distrust of the banking system.

- Some individuals don't have enough money to meet the minimum requirements of a bank.

- Illegal immigrants may not have the paperwork needed to open a bank account.

Some cryptocurrencies aim to help the unbanked by allowing them to store, use, and transfer their money with few requirements.

It's very easy for someone to look at the list above and say, "Well if you're an illegal immigrant, of course you shouldn't be able to open a bank account."

Or, "The minimum requirements are there for a reason! If they don't meet them, they're out of luck." In my opinion, this is wrong for a few reasons.

Let's look at the minimum requirements first. In the USA it's almost certain that you'll meet the minimum requirements such as age, having the proper ID, and having the minimum amount of capital to open an account. However, it's not that certain in other countries. Especially ones that are developing.

ID issuance is a service performed by a government. For that to happen, a country must have a working government. What if a country's government is not functional? What if a child is born in a rural part of the country and slips through the cracks? It's entirely possible that child grows up with no ID.

In the USA, we have the luxury and obligation to send our children to school up until a certain age. In some places that age is lower, if it even exists at all. Many boys in other countries are considered grown men as early as 12 or 13 years old. This same young individual may work on a family farm and sell produce to the local markets.

Now, if that same person wants to open a bank account to start saving money to purchase tools and equipment to make their production more efficient, they could be out of luck if they don't have the required documents that often times only well-off people have!

Say this individual discovers that trading surplus produce with nearby towns would be more efficient if they hired a courier. This person would like to take out a loan using his savings as collateral to grow his business. But he has no credit score and is technically non-existent to the credit system just because he never had a bank account or a credit card.

So how can this hardworking and creative child move out of his current economic situation without banking services? What about the universal right of the pursuit of happiness? For this person, it doesn't exist, and the system inherently limits him. This applies to billions of people around the world today.

Crypto could be the tool for some of these individuals where the system has failed them. When they need a loan, they could use services like SALT, MakerDAO, or another system that provides loans on crypto collateral and doesn't care if you are a 12-year-old in Kenya, or a 40-year-old in Manhattan. In crypto, we are all equal. As long as you control the private keys to a crypto wallet, you can get loans against that crypto. By its nature, crypto is unable to discriminate.

Today, thanks to crypto, much of the world's limited access to basic financial services can be accomplished with a smartphone, Internet connection, and a bit of education.

*If you would like to see the alt-coins we're trading in **real-time**, you can do so at crypto101insider.com.*

Section 02

Joining The Crypto Revolution and Becoming a Crypto Crusader

As told by Bryce...

Cryptocurrency lives outside the current money system. It is a brand-new system. And anyone with an Internet connection can join in the thriving crypto market. That's the point.

But how do you know where to start? And how do you do so safely? As you will soon see, the world of cryptocurrency has different rules than the fiat world you're used to. This is not inherently a good or bad thing, it's just something you must understand before you actually trade your fiat currency for crypto citizenship.

First, you need to understand that Bitcoin isn't the only coin. In fact, at the time of this writing, there are an estimated 177,000 ERC-20 token contracts in the world.[87] Each one is fighting to claim a stake in the future of money, and it's a beautiful thing!

Bitcoin, right now, is the "gold standard" crypto. It was the first fully decentralized one, and has been around the longest. It has also proven resilient, weathering bubbles, threats of regulation, government attack and more.

In 2013, a Google developer named Charlie Lee made a "hard fork" of Bitcoin, changed some parameters, and created a new coin… Litecoin.

Unlike Bitcoin, which allows for just 21 million tokens generated, ever, Litecoin allows for 84 million.[88] Litecoin also has a different consensus algorithm securing the network, and faster transaction speed. It isn't objectively better or worse, it is just different and plays a different role (almost like the silver to Bitcoin's "gold").

On the contrary, it does have objectively less hash power securing the network, and less liquidity on the exchanges, but so does EVERY other crypto. But it is objectively faster to send. Without getting too technical, Bitcoin's slowness

(10 min block time compared to Litecoin's 2.5 minutes) is actually a function of its security.

Obviously, this industry is still incredibly new and anything could happen. I'm telling you this to illustrate how different coins can serve different purposes. Here's what they all have in common: they revolve around the bank account of the future. The human being. YOU!

With everything we've gone over so far in this book, you're probably feeling optimistic about digital currency. And that's great because there is so much to be optimistic about. And, think of it this way, most of the really amazing tech that's going to be using blockchain hasn't even been *thought* of yet.

So, you see crypto and where it's going. And now that I'm talking about being your own bank, you're probably feeling pretty good about that, too. You're probably feeling good about living in a world that isn't controlled by a tiny handful of elites who are pulling the levers on the money printers.

BUT…

We need to have a little talk.

I want to make absolutely sure you know what this means. Because the reality is, yes, we are ruled by people who control the money. But, in return, *we don't really have to worry about it that much.*

If you make a purchase online and they don't deliver the product, you can call your bank and get a chargeback. If, God forbid, the bank loses $10,000 you were storing with them, they're insured. You can get it back.

If you lose your bank password, you can reset it.

Yes, when the next recession hits caused by prolonged artificially low interest rates, Fractional Reserve lending and Quantitative Easing, you very well may lose your job. You very well may lose much of your savings and any investments you had in the market.

However, *until that point,* the current system makes things easy for us in our day-to-day lives. Awfully convenient.

Right now, the crypto infrastructure isn't fully there— herein also lies the financial opportunity! In other words, if you buy something with Bitcoin and they don't deliver, tough luck. Maybe you can leave a negative review. But there won't be any third-party operator who can bail you out.

In just a second, we're going to be talking about a VERY important topic: your "Private Key". This is so important, that if you forget it, or even just forget to write it down when you're prompted to, **you may lose access to your crypto completely, forever.**

I'm serious.

It's estimated that over 3.72 million Bitcoin have been lost from the Earth *forever*. How are they destroyed or lost? In the early days, people hardly valued Bitcoin—they mined lots of Bitcoin as an experiment, but then threw away that old hard drive where the private keys were stored. Or they deleted their files where the Bitcoin private keys were stored. Or they transferred the Bitcoin to a non-existent address which results in them being lost in the ether forever! Or they lost their keys and are unable to access them!

At $10,000 per Bitcoin, thats $37.2 BILLION that's been removed circulation, and makes the Bitcoin you own today, a bit more valuable.[89]

Now, you may be wondering, if crypto is so easy to lose, how is it possible that it can be the currency of the future? After all, we've all had a situation where the bank has bailed us out. If that doesn't exist, can crypto really ever take over?

Look… this is a book about getting in early.

The people who have *already* made fortunes with crypto got in *really* early, even before a lot of the conveniences we have in the space today. The risk was an order of magnitude higher, so it only makes sense that the rewards they reaped were, too. If they bought Bitcoin 10 years ago when it first hit exchanges, an initial $1,000 investment would be worth over $35,000,000. In 10 years.

Up until now, the message I've been trying to get across to you more than anything is this:

We are still in the early days!

I don't have a crystal ball. But I've loaded heaps of evidence on you to show you just how early it still is. And the past 10 years of crypto are TINY in comparison with what the next 10 years will *most likely* be.

So the biggest gains go to the people who embrace the new technology—the new future—before others even realize it's happening.

The most money is always made in the "Wild West" phase. So as an early crypto investor, someone who sees the future before it's here, that's something you need to prepare for.

The Wild West is almost gone. Actual real banks in Europe are now offering cryptocurrencies to their customers. Governing bodies all the way up to the United Nations are passing laws and guidelines about sending and taxing crypto. Centralized platforms are insured against losses, but not against governments demanding consumer data or court orders to freeze assets.

But we will have a long way to go for the user experience across crypto to be ready for everybody to use comfortably. If you are looking for a system of money that is RIGHT NOW more convenient than fiat, a system that has had millennia to develop...

Stop reading this book right now! We're not there yet.

Now, let me show you the other side of the coin. Because the truth is, even though crypto is still not quite as convenient as fiat, it's getting astonishingly close. And it comes with all kinds of advantages that fiat doesn't. For example, as long as you have your private key and no one else does, you can access your crypto in any country in the world, on any phone, or computer that's connected to the

Internet. If you remember and keep your mnemonic phrase and private key safe, no matter where you are in the world, you can trade, send and receive digital currency in seconds.

But if you're the kind of person who is constantly breaking their phone, losing their wallet -- don't worry. There are safe, secure platforms for allowing a third-party (custodian) to hold the private keys instead. We can't recommend this, because as the saying goes, "not your keys, not your crypto" However, it has become a much more valid option in recent months than it ever has been before. Crypto custodians are worth mentioning now, so more people have a chance to comfortably participate. More on custodians like Coinbase later.

What's a Crypto Crusader?

In the next part of this book, I'll show you how to buy your very first crypto. But before we even get there, I'm going to ask you an important question:

Are you a Crypto Crusader?

If you're not sure, it's okay. Here are the typical traits of people who have gone all-in with crypto. Crypto Crusaders are usually:

Global Citizens

Crypto Crusaders want to divorce themselves from elite-controlled fiat systems. They want the freedom to buy and sell without government interference or the restriction of borders. They often dream about traveling the world with just a private key, using crypto as their go-to currency.

Entrepreneurial

Crypto Crusaders are eager to explore new technologies, take everything they've learned, and build something of their own. They aim to live life to the fullest, creating new projects, new companies, and new business opportunities.

Passionate About the future

Infinitely curious, Crypto Crusaders love learning about future tech. They're usually the first to know about scientific breakthroughs, and can't wait to tell others about their theories. They're typically optimistic about what humanity is capable of.

Risk-Tolerant

While this book is all about safe investing, Crypto Crusaders are somewhat risk-tolerant. They understand that any investment carries risk, so they're mostly calm about the peaks and valleys of the crypto market.

Focused on the Long-Term

Many Crypto Crusaders know that perfecting blockchain technology could take time. So they typically invest in projects that may take at least a decade to develop, and they're fine with waiting to see things come to fruition.

The people who made the most money in the crypto market invested almost 10 years ago. This book is about taking a long-term strategy with crypto.

In other words, if you find yourself constantly saying "when moon?" or "when lambo?", and you're looking to get rich quick, this book probably isn't for you.

The Crypto Crusader Manifesto

A Crypto Crusader is a progressive individual. Smarter, Wiser, in-Control and Free

Crypto Crusaders wage guerrilla war against greedy corporations.
And WIN.

Crypto Crusaders start without waiting for inefficient governments.
"Procrastination" is a four-letter word and "Action" is their middle name.

Crypto Crusaders never give up control, because

Their wealth stays in their hands—Not a wasteful government.

Crypto Crusaders never ask for permission and are never enslaved to a bank.

A Crypto Crusader generates wealth and takes back power, but doesn't abuse it.

If you ask the MBAs or look at your college textbooks, They'll tell you that what you're doing is impossible…Yet the wave has already started and it's not stopping.

Crypto Crusaders
Generate Their Own Wealth.
Move their money freely.
Believe in transparency.
Are a part of the future.

Crypto Crusaders are motivated knowing that they are One Decision Away.

I AM A CRYPTO CRUSADER

Get "Over the Shoulder" Access to Our Entire Crypto Portfolio… and Follow Our Exact Trades, Step-By-Step at **crypto101insider.com**

19

7 Instant Benefits You'll Gain From Using Crypto

As told by Bryce...

It's easy to look at cryptocurrency as a long-term investment vehicle. And, it can certainly serve that purpose. Remember though, the point of crypto is not to simply raise in price over the long run. It's to take over, and ultimately replace, the current banking and finance systems.

As you know by now, different forms of money and currency are always fighting each other for dominance. The more powerful the currency, the better and more conveniently it stores value, the more advantages people who use that currency will have.

Although I speak a lot about using crypto for investing in this book, the reality is you can start seeing the amazing benefits of cryptocurrency right away.

Investing in crypto isn't about only the long-term. It's about plugging yourself into a brand-new financial system right away. And although the fiat system of dollars and cents is, initially, more convenient, with crypto citizenship comes an entirely new level of power and freedom you've never experienced before. So, before we get into how to *invest* in crypto, I want to show you 7 different ways you can benefit from your crypto the very second you buy it.

Benefit #1: Access to Global Talent

The book you are reading is the result of hardworking people all over the world. Imagine you are a small business owner, and you contract people from all over the world. You have a writer in Australia, a designer in Indonesia, a bookkeeper in the United Kingdom…

You are all already tied together through the Internet. Why then are transactions between honest, hardworking citizens across national borders so difficult?

Using crypto, you can pay someone, no matter where they are in the world. From there they could cash out into their local currency at the current exchange rate, or choose to hold onto a portion, or all of it, as an investment.

Sourcing Work Globally

Thanks to crypto, now everyone on the planet can have their own global team. One example of this in action is a new website called www.bounties.network. Similar to TaskRabbit or Fiverr, Bounties Network allows you to set a "bounty" for any kind of work you want done: logo or website design, writing, branding, marketing, anything you can think of!

Anyone who browses the website, from anywhere in the world, can then send in a submission for the contest. You can then choose whichever submission you like the most. Thanks to smart contracts, the moment you choose the one you like, the person who created it gets paid.

Although this kind of service is young, blockchain is already allowing capital to be distributed to anywhere in the world. All with no middleman. Trustless—you don't need to trust that the person opposite of you will hold up their end of the bargain. The blockchain and smart contract *is* the escrow agent.

Benefit #2: Instant Payments Without Friction

This is the obvious benefit. The value inherent in being able to send money to anyone, anywhere in the world at a moment's notice is pretty self-evident. All while paying virtually nothing in fees.

This is the kind of benefit that you don't know you need until you need it. It is important that you know and remember this fact about crypto, so that if a situation does come up where you need this ability, you have it!

Maybe a family member of yours gets into an accident and is in a hospital abroad. You relative's life is on the line and they need surgery, but the hospital needs payment upfront. If the surgery is time-sensitive, wire transfers would be too slow, and bank branches in that area might not be able to accept incoming wires from your particular bank. You could send them crypto and arrange an immediate cash out through an exchange or peer-to-peer transaction nearby.

Benefit #3: Rewire Your Brain

The fact is, the majority of people live their lives without knowing *anything* about future tech, until it falls in their lap. Most people are late-adopters, and that's fine.

However, these late adopters miss out on all the amazing opportunity that comes along with riding the wave of technology *before* it reaches mainstream appeal. For example, if you were in-tune with e-commerce and online shopping, you would've seen Amazon's rise long before most others. As a result you could've invested in Amazon stock early on and made a fortune.

Blockchain and crypto are a key part of the future. And when you plug yourself into this kind of mindset, you start to get deeply involved in the future personally. Not only will this lead to new convenience in your life, as you are able to use new technologies before most even know about them, you're also in a prime position to invest and benefit financially from them.

Benefit #4: A Business or Career in Blockchain

As you know by now, the world of blockchain is growing at a rapid pace. Many of the top Fortune 500 companies are personally investing in blockchain technology. And the demand is only going to increase.

Think about it this way. Imagine you were a lawyer that just passed the bar exam, looking to start your own practice. What do you think would be a faster route to success?

1. Opening a DUI practice in your city, which already has several established firms who handle these exact cases

2. Opening a practice that focuses exclusively on helping businesses replace written contracts with

smart contract systems

The truth is, many of the "tried and true" industries of the past are now saturated with more talent than the industry can absorb. There simply isn't enough demand to meet the supply of talent. And, there isn't as much room for upside in those older industries anymore.

Not so with blockchain.

The field is wide open, and the opportunity is plentiful.

For most of my life, people have told me they enjoy hearing my stories and experiences. So podcasting was a natural career path for me. Had I done it on something else I enjoy, like playing guitar or sports, it only *might've* worked out. However, since I did it in crypto and blockchain, a wide open space, I was able to ride the technology wave and it's worked out very well. It's the reason you're holding this book in your hands right now.

Thinking back, there's no question in my mind that working for companies in the crypto space and building a crypto podcast has shaved time off of my journey towards financial freedom. It can do the same for you.

If you're an entrepreneur and interested in starting a new business, or expanding your current one, look to crypto and blockchain. If you're looking to upgrade your career, look to crypto and blockchain.

Benefit #5: Intellectual Property on the Blockchain

This one is for creative types: artists, musicians, architects —anyone who handles intellectual property. The last thing you want to do is create a masterpiece that anyone can steal without giving you any royalties or credit.

Unfortunately, this is exactly what's been happening ever since the beginning of time. Oftentimes, the original creator is left to rot in the dust while someone else profits from their life's work.

Once again, blockchain to the rescue.

Writing a *smart* creative license into an NFT (non-fungible token), artists can now create true *digital* originals of their art and have programmatic royalties paid out every time an action is done to that digital file.

For instance, the NFT could be a song or a music video. That creator of the original file can code into the smart contract that governs the file, that every time someone wants to view it, no matter where it ends up on the internet, they need to pay 5 cents, for example. And when they do pay that 5 cents, 4 cents needs to go back to a wallet address owned by the creator, giving the creator the rightful majority share.

Because of this, artists are now able to create digital art, host it on a smart contract platform like Ethereum, and monetize it! What's more, this digital art has actual value that can increase, just like physical art in the real world. In fact, I predict that some of the most expensive goods in the world will be pieces of digital art, in the same way that people collect and auction off physical art. We are already starting to see markets form around digital art on platforms like SuperRare and RareArt.

Moreover, there was a phenomenon called CryptoKitties, a game where you collect digital cats that range from ultra-ultra rare to common. At its peak, the most expensive CryptoKitty was bought for 600 Ether, or about $170,000.

Everyone knows that becoming a famous musician is almost impossible. One of the most surefire ways to get there is to write a hit. Problem is, writing a hit is expensive. So millions of talented artists out there are never even able to try.

Well, what if you could invest in an artist? You could search for them and, if you liked their music, contribute a percentage of the amount they need to record it, in exchange for a bit of ownership. The artist can then record their song professionally.

If it blows up, since you bought a percentage of the NFT (which is the digital representation of their album, for instance), you will earn a percentage of those royalties. Blockchain is going to usher in a new art renaissance with millions of patrons.

Benefit #6: Sense of Community and Like Mindedness

Probably my favorite part about getting involved in crypto is all the new friends and amazing people I've met. The blockchain and crypto community is tight knit, with people all over the world. Getting involved in a community that is totally forward-thinking is going to benefit your life in ways you can't imagine right now.

For example, I mentioned that some of the biggest supporters of life extension work are also Crypto Crusaders. When you plug into the crypto community, you start learning all kinds of amazing knowledge that you'd never find anywhere else. You stop waiting for the future, and you participate in it actively.

You meet all kinds of people exactly like you. Your tribe. People who are sick of working so hard only to have governments devalue their currency or banks loaning their money out to projects they don't approve of. People who don't want to be afraid of the future, but want to profit and benefit from it instead.

People who want their own stake in the future. And to have their thumbprints and ideas helping to form and support the early stages.

It's a melting pot of people who know an awful lot about all kinds of industries. This is a community that can provide everything from emotional support to a life-changing job or business opportunity.

Benefit #7: Inspiration and Hope

This may be a benefit you don't expect. Yet for me, it's the cornerstone of why I've invested into crypto and blockchain. The truth is, even though we have it better than just about every other human being to ever exist, we're still born into a rigged system. It's all been set up by people we don't know. And for the most part, we haven't had any real say in how any of it should work.

Sure, you can vote, which is a major improvement over monarchies and dictatorships. But we all know how slow government can work. Even if the person you vote for makes it into office, the odds that anything significant will change is very unlikely. *The fact is, the system we're using is outdated.* Blockchain is the better option—one that is automated, instant, entirely digital, and secure.

Moreover, blockchain is *outside* of the current system. It's not something that has to be ran through a committee or approved by some overall governing force. It exists independently.

And it's the foundation for an entire infrastructure of tools that can be used without relying on middlemen, people in power, or anything other than electricity, computing power, the internet, and individual users. Money and government are two examples of systems that control almost everything we do—two examples of systems we have virtually no control over—*systems that can be done better on the blockchain.*

In a blockchain world, everyone has a voice. Everyone has genuine, true independence and freedom. We are no longer forced to trust ruling bodies who most likely do not have our best interests in mind. Governments of the future being built on blockchain is one of the most powerful and disruptive ideas born out of crypto. I think it will happen slowly and gradually, but it is inevitable if the governed (me and you) will it into existence.

Therefore, I no longer worry about what the future holds, because I'm helping to create it. I no longer feel helpless and depressed when something political happens that I disagree with. Sure, a blockchain world isn't here today. But in 10-20 years, it will be. And I'll have played a vital role in making sure that happens. It gives me hope and purpose. If you're like that, if you have the makeup of a Crypto Crusader, I know it will do the same for you.

20

There Are Levels To This

As told by Bryce...

If you've reached this point, then you've decided that you're responsible enough to get into the Wild West of crypto. And you're ready to build a safety net and financial foundation *outside* of the current fiat system.

I've been trying to scare you a little bit up until this point. And that's for good reason: truly, this isn't for everyone! And if you're *not* the kind of person who can succeed in crypto, I would be doing you an ENORMOUS disservice by making it seem easy.

So, here's the good news:

You can take on as much responsibility as you want.

There are levels to the crypto game.

So, let's start at the top.

Crypto Exchanges

The first level is the crypto exchange. This is where you can exchange your dollars, euros, pounds, yen, or any other global fiat currency, for crypto. You can buy one of the more popular coins like Bitcoin, Litecoin or Ethereum. Or, you can buy one of the up-and-comers like EOS, Chainlink, or Zcash.

And, that can be it for you. You can buy $500 worth of Bitcoin, Litecoin and Ethereum. You can then keep that money on the exchange. You can totally forget about it, and 10 years later, you can log back in and collect your riches.

...most likely, at least.

I say most likely because some of the largest exchanges in the world have been hacked and stolen from. In the largest hack, the Mt. Gox hack, over $400,000,000 worth of crypto was stolen.[90] Imagine realizing 10 years in the future that your investment has paid off huge, only to check your exchange account and see it's not there.

That's why in the crypto world, we say if you keep your crypto on the exchange, *you don't really own any.* We've said it before and we will say it again: "Not your keys, not your crypto." It basically means that if you're not storing your crypto on a wallet where you own both the public and private keys, it's not really YOUR money. And you're also not receiving any of the advantages that come with owning it yourself.

Which is why we strongly recommend you advance to the next level, and take on a little bit more responsibility.

Software Wallets (Hot Wallet)

There are dozens of high-quality software wallets that allow you to store any crypto you buy on an exchange. But, there's a catch: In order to use these wallets, you need to keep track of your **private key**.

Please, please, please: pay attention here as this is extremely important!

I will be walking you through this step. But when you first open a software wallet, you will be told a 12 or 24-word mnemonic which generates your private key. You MUST write these words down and store them in a safe place! (I will be telling you where you can store it to keep it safe soon.)

As long as you have access to this mnemonic, you can access your crypto from anywhere in the world, from any wallet that exists, on any phone or computer that can connect to the Internet. This is the step that literally turns you into your own personal human bank account!

You can easily transfer crypto off the exchange and into your software wallet by pasting your new wallet's public address into the "send" field on the exchange. This makes it exponentially safer.

That being said, as long as the device that knows your private keys (i.e. your phone) is connected to the Internet, there is a *very slim* chance that some very clever bad actor could hack your wallet and drain your crypto.

So, for people who want to be extra safe, that takes us to the next level, where the device that knows your private keys is *offline* meaning it has never touched the internet, and never will be able to.

Hardware Wallets/Cold Storage

You can easily take the money you've stored in software wallet and transfer it to a hardware wallet. This is like a USB stick, but it's *much* more secure.

It's also not connected to the Internet. So, you can download all your crypto onto it, disconnect it, and all of it will stay on the hardware wallet and no malware snooping on your network, phone, or computer can ever see your private keys. Even if every phone and computer you ever own or touch is hacked, which is unlikely to say the least, your crypto will be 100% protected.

21

Taking The Plunge

As told by Bryce...

In this chapter, I'm going to guide you down the first three levels. I'm going to illustrate a few different investable options. We're going to start with the "blue chips" of crypto. These are the major coins that, while still volatile, are a lot more trustworthy than any of the thousands of altcoins available.

Exchanges: Your Gateway to Crypto

The first step to adding your first crypto to your wallet is to join an exchange. The exchange that I chose to walk you through and serve as your on ramp into the world of crypto is called Coinbase. Founded in 2012, Coinbase has over 20,000,000 active users who have traded over $150 billion on the platform.[91]

For this reason, it's the first place I recommend you set up your account. But first…

Just How Secure Is Coinbase?

Due to its open, decentralized infrastructure, cryptocurrency has a lot going for it by way of security. Bitcoin is the hardest thing on earth to hack right now.

However, exchanges crypto is traded on *have* been hacked. Therefore, I want to spend some time talking about how secure Coinbase is, so you can know your investment is safe.

Also, in the start of this section, I talked about how at this moment, banks and traditional money are still more convenient than crypto. But in this section, you'll see: *crypto is catching up quickly.* In fact, Coinbase has many security features that your online bank doesn't. So let's take a look at what makes this exchange so secure!

Offline Storage

Coinbase stores approximately 98% of its crypto *offline.*[92] This makes it very difficult to hack because there is no easy way for a hack or virus to spread across the network. Instead, the only way a hacker could actually gain access to the coin is if they were able to breach multiple physical locations, all protected by state-of-the-art, military-grade security systems.

Coinbase further increases security by storing all its crypto in multiple locations around the world.

Data Storage

Coinbase also stores your sensitive data offline, going as far as encrypting your data before copying it onto paper backups and military-grade, secured USB drives. These paper backups and USB drives are also distributed around the world to physical locations, making it almost impossible for anyone with bad intent to gain access to.

Multi-Factor Verification

Coinbase requires all users to use a two-step verification process, which you must go through at least once every 30 days to use the platform. This two-step process requires all users to enter a code from their mobile phone when logging in. In other words, to breach your account, not only would someone need to have your username and password, they would also need to have access to your phone at the moment they're logging in to your online account.

Also, if you sign in from a new IP or location that Coinbase doesn't recognize as associated with your account, they'll send you an email as well as a code you need to enter in from your mobile phone.

To make your account even more secure, we recommend using a service like Google Authenticator. You need to download it on your iOS or Android device. The problem with using SMS alone is if someone steals your phone and gains access through a SIM Swap or theft, they immediately gain access to your email and phone. So a text message isn't really going to stop them at that point.

However, with Google Authenticator, you need to enter a separate password to even go through the verification process. This adds another level of security that makes it exponentially harder for anyone who isn't you to gain access to your account.

The Human Element

Although advanced security measures like the ones described can make it very difficult—if not impossible— for a hacker to steal your funds, the possibility of human error must also be accounted for.

Coinbase handles this by putting every employee through a detailed criminal background check. All hardware used by these employees is secured by bank-level encryption, and employees are required to use incredibly strong passwords. (I'll show you how to come up with and remember your own strong password shortly.)

FDIC Insured

In Coinbase, you fund your account with US dollars (or other accepted currency). During this time, you'll have USD stored on Coinbase. Although cryptocurrency is currently not insured by the federal government, the cash balance you have on the exchange is up to $250,000!

Regulated By The U.S. Government

Because Coinbase handles such a large volume of cash transactions, it is regulated by the same government agencies that regulate banks. It has a license for money transmission in every state it operates in. And it's also licensed with FinCEN as a Money Services Business.

Questions about how to set up your crypto securely? Interested in knowing about the top coins before they're released? Learn more at crypto101insider.com

22

Keeping Yourself Secure

As told by Aaron...

The platform of Coinbase is incredibly secure. That being said, it's all for nothing if you give away sensitive details. Remember that Coinbase customer service will NEVER ask you for details such as the all-important Private Key. If you *do* need to contact customer support, make sure you are ONLY using the email or phone number found on Coinbase.com.

How to Create (and Remember) a Strong Password

Password DON'Ts:

- Do NOT use words like "password" or "secret"

- Do NOT use personal information like hometown, school name, significant other's name, or anything someone close to you could readily guess

- Do NOT use words from the dictionary

- Do NOT use basic keyboard patterns like "qwerty"

Password DOs:

- Use uppercase and lowercase letters

- Use numbers

- Use symbols

- Have a password length of at *least* 12 characters

How to Create an Ultra-Strong Password (That's Easy to Remember)

Recently, the CEO of QuadrigaCX, a large crypto exchange, died. *And the company private key died with him*. As a result, over $190,000,000 in cryptocurrency was lost for good![93]

The moral? Even the strongest password is useless if it's lost and forgotten.

Never fear: Today I'm going to show you a quick and easy way to generate a strong password that you can easily remember, too.

First, take any random sentence. It could be:

- Cryptocurrency is going to take over the world

- When AI takes over, they will be using cryptocurrency to earn money

- I need to take my dog out before I go to bed tonight

- ...or anything else you can think of

(REMEMBER: THIS BOOK WILL BE READ BY A LEGION OF PEOPLE. MAKE UP YOUR OWN SENTENCE, PLEASE!)

Let's use the first sentence: Cryptocurrency is going to take over the world

Here is the secure password, or *cipher,* I created using this sentence:

Cc$Ig2tOtW!!

How? I took the first word, cryptocurrency, and used it to start my password: Cc. Then I added a $ symbol. Next a capital "I" for "is." A lowercase "g" for "going." The number "2" for "to." A lowercase "t" for "take." An uppercase "O" for "over." Another lowercase "t" for "the." An uppercase "W" for "world." Followed by two exclamation points.

We now have a password that uses upper and lowercase letters, numbers, and symbols. I can also remember it relatively easily, after practicing it a few times.

Although this kind of password is easier for *you* to remember, it's impossible for someone to guess. And because of its length and complexity, it's also virtually impossible for a hacker to "bruteforce" guess it with software, no matter how sophisticated.

Coinbase and other exchanges also limit the number of login attempts you can make, so brute-forcing actually *is* impossible.

Automating Your Passwords

Since this is a book about the future, I wanted to include automated ways you can generate and store secure passwords.

By using a simple website like https://passwordsgenerator.net/, you can instantly generate a complex password 16 characters in length or longer.

Changing Your Password Every Six Months

If you truly want to take your security to the next level, I recommend changing your passwords every 6 months. When you generate a strong password, you may use it on multiple websites, some of which don't have the security that Coinbase does. If one of these other sites gets compromised, a hacker could then use that same password on your Coinbase account.

You can set a reminder on your calendar to change your password every 90 days. You can then use https://passwordsgenerator.net/ to generate a new password. Finally, by using LastPass (https://www.lastpass.com), you can store every one of these passwords securely.

LastPass allows you to pick ONE "master password." Every time you use that one password, it will enter the correct password on the website you're in. For example, your LastPass master could be "crypto1014Life!." And your Coinbase password could be "vrr@9dx7U$[p&RQ$." By simply entering "crypto1014Life!" on Coinbase, LastPass will enter in "vrr@9dx7U$[p&RQ$."..or whatever your latest password for that site is.

This allows you to be as secure as possible without having to remember a ton of crazy passwords.

23

How To Sign Up For Coinbase

As told by Aaron...

Now that we have security out the way, let's actually get you set up with your first Coinbase account, and buy your first crypto.

First, open your web browser and go to https:// www.Coinbase.com

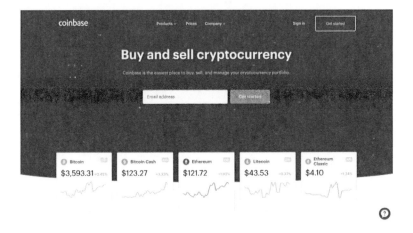

Click "Get started" in the upper right-hand corner.

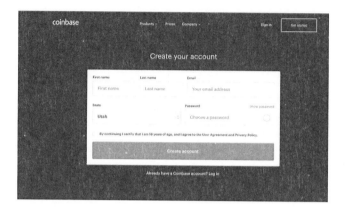

Fill it out completely and use the strong password I taught you to make in the previous section.

Go to the email you used and find the email from Coinbase:

Once you verify your email, you'll be asked to enter a phone number. This is for the two-step verification we discussed earlier, so make sure it's a primary number you will be using for a long time.

Add your phone number

Country

🇺🇸 United States

Your Phone Number

+1 |__ - ___ - ____

This will secure your account by texting a short confirmation code to your phone when logging in.

Send Code

After you've verified your phone, you'll need to verify your identity to comply with federal regulations. Remember: your data is safer on Coinbase than just about any other website on the planet.

Financial regulations require us to verify your identity. Once complete, you can buy, sell or transfer digital currency. Learn more.

First Name	Last Name	What will you use Coinbase for?
First Name	Last Name	

Date of Birth

What is your source of funds?

Street Address

Current Occupation

123 Main Street

Unit #

Employer

Employer

City/town   Utah

Last 4 digits of SSN

ZIP code   Country
United States of America   1234

Continue

In the next step, you'll be prompted to enter your credit card and Bank Account. A credit card allows you to immediately buy crypto. A bank account will take some time to verify, but once it's verified, you'll have a higher limit on the amount you can buy at any one time.

Congratulations! You now have a Coinbase account. Here's what your screen should look like:

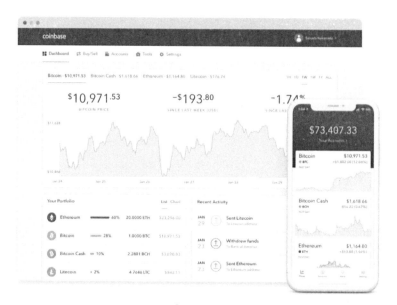

At the top of your dashboard are the prices for three of the top coins, Bitcoin, Ethereum and Litecoin. You can see the price from hourly, daily, weekly, monthly or yearly increments. Once you buy crypto, you will also see the worth of your account updated on a daily basis.

If you want to see the full status of your account, and receive and send money to others, click on the "Accounts" tab.

Using Google Authenticator or Authy

As mentioned earlier, to further secure your account, I highly recommend using either Google Authenticator (for Android users) or Authy (for everyone).

Enabling this extra level of security is easy. Simply navigate to Settings -> Security. Then click "Enable Authenticator":

Your two-factor method is: SMS

For more security, enable an authenticator app.

Type in the code Coinbase sends to your phone. Then follow the instructions to connect your authenticator program to Coinbase:

Buying Your First "Blue Chip" Cryptos

In traditional investing, a "Blue Chip" stock is a company that has been around for a long time, and is likely to stay around for a long time.

Companies like Apple, Coca-Cola, Nike, Disney, etc.

Investing in these stocks is unlikely to make you wealthy overnight. So why invest in them? Because over time, they've been shown to gain a MASSIVE amount.

Crypto has its own "blue chip" cryptos. They are: Bitcoin, Ethereum, and Litecoin.

Although the world of crypto is still very new, these three coins have weathered many up-and-down cycles and remain on top. But there's something different about these three coins that I want you to look at: *each one has considerably evolved technology with its creation.*

First you have Bitcoin. The original. With Bitcoin came the blockchain and open ledger. Bitcoin brought trust by consensus.

Then you have Ethereum. Created by Vitalik Buterin, Ethereum is the world's first dApp platform. Simply put, a dApp is a decentralized app. It's an application that can actually use the blockchain to make your own app.

Then, lastly, there is Litecoin. Litecoin, as the name implies, is a lighter, faster version of Bitcoin. It also offers far lower transaction costs, usually just a couple of pennies regardless of transaction amount. (In one famous transaction, over $62,000,000 worth of Litecoin was transferred for just 50 cents!).

Now, because we're investing in crypto, these three coins are still VERY volatile. However, since they have the largest adoption, they do have some stability when compared to the rest of the smaller coins, so it is good to keep these in your portfolio.

Additionally, they are the coins that *could* see the largest increase in price in a new bull market (which could come about due to new tech, government regulation, or any number of reasons discussed in this book).

Although you'll be hard-pressed to find a bigger believer in blockchain than me, even I will admit that investing is a risk. We just don't know what's going to happen. That's why I'm very firm in saying you should NEVER invest money you can't afford to lose into crypto.

That being said, if you do have money lying around that you want to invest in a future that is very real—and very much on its way—I think it is prudent to have a portion of your money in crypto. And I would also say it's unwise to have zero exposure to this new emerging asset class—there simply is no industry on the planet that is shaping up to change our day-to-day lives like crypto.

24

Storing Crypto In A Wallet

As told by Aaron...

In the beginning of crypto, storing was pretty difficult. You needed a separate wallet for every different coin you had. And since most investors were looking to invest in multiple alt-coins, they'd need to remember the information for a ton of different wallets.

Nowadays though, it's much simpler. Although you still need a wallet for each different coin you have, you can store all these wallets under one main account. Here are a few of the wallets that let you do that:

Trust Wallet

Trust Wallet is the wallet owned by the largest crypto exchange in the world, Binance. It can hold Bitcoin and Ethereum coins, over 20,000 different options in total. It's intuitive, works on iPhone and Android, and has many different security features:

- Server-free environment fully localizes each installed application

- Client-based infrastructure ensures that keys are stored locally, on your device

- Bank-level security safeguards your digital assets from potential threats

- Application-level authentication system prevents anyone from accessing your wallet...even if your device is unlocked

(Taken from TrustWallet.com)

Coinbase Wallet

You're already familiar with Coinbase from buying your first coins. They also have a wallet solution for storage. It comes with many of the same security features as Trust Wallet.

Atomic Wallet

This is a strong wallet with a convenient and beautiful user interface. Some crypto veterans want to spread out their investments as much as possible. So, if you need an additional wallet after Coinbase and Trust, Atomic is a phenomenal option.

I think Trust Wallet is the best, so that's the one I'm going to use to demonstrate. And I'll be walking you through every step of the way. You'll go through a very similar process to set up other wallets—They're all designed to be easy to set up.

Remember...the most important part is your PRIVATE KEY. When the wallet tells you your private key—or tells you to back it up—*do it*, and write down, keep track and securely store it.

25

How To Set Up Your Trust Wallet

As told by Aaron...

First, depending on if you have an iPhone or Android, you'll want to open the App Store or Google Play store respectively. Please refer to Trust Wallet's website [https://www.trustwallet.com] for the latest set up instructions that may have been altered since the time of publishing.

9:00 ⏱

‏‏ ▇

< Search

Trust - Ethereum Wallet

Private & Secure Wallet

⟲ ⋯

4.5 ★★★★⯪   4+
230 Ratings   Age

What's New   Version History

Version 1.1.121   5d ago

- Watch any wallet on the blockchain, just add it
on the import screen.
- Increased gas price and gas limits.   more

Preview

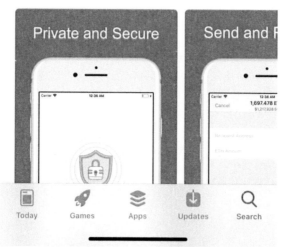

Today   Games   Apps   Updates   Search

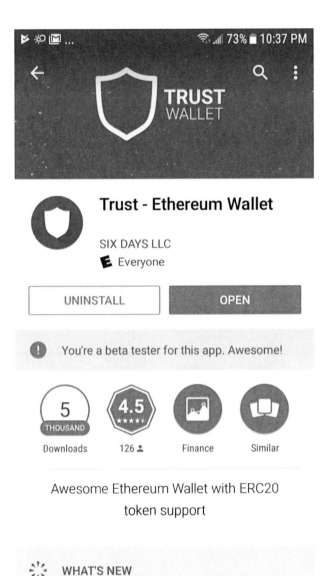

Download the app. Open it up and you'll see this screen:

Private & Secure

Private keys never leave your device

• · · ·

Click on "Create Wallet."

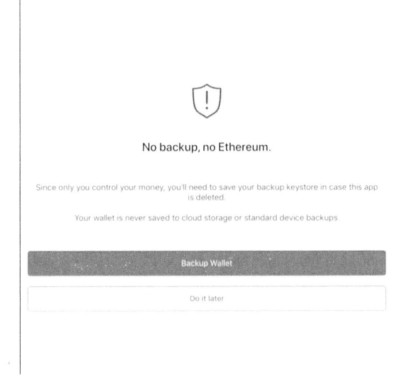

No backup, no Ethereum.

Since only you control your money, you'll need to save your backup keystore in case this app is deleted.

Your wallet is never saved to cloud storage or standard device backups

Backup Wallet

Do it later

Once you create your wallet you can then locate your public keys and start receiving the various cryptocurrencies their platform allows.

26

Your First Coinbase Purchase

As told by Aaron...

Once you make the decision to "buy in" to the future, and become a crypto citizen, actually making the purchase is safe and easy. In a way, almost *too* safe and too easy. Because it will remind you of using your bank's website. All the choices are right in front of you and taking action is a piece of cake. Still, I'll be guiding you every step of the way.

But please, please, please, *do not forget the importance of BEING YOUR OWN BANK.*

You need to keep your private key secret above everything. No matter what happens, do NOT give it up to ANYONE. No matter how official it looks!

The fact is, every single day millions of dollars in crypto is stolen. You can think it'll never happen to you, but believe me, it can. And if you go in ignorant, it will.

It's happened to many of my friends who are genuinely smart people. They get careless. They make a mistake. They lose their money. Don't let it happen to you—*keep your private key safe!*

Now, your *public* key, on the other hand, you can be much more lenient about. Yet keep in mind that there are ways people can track your address back to you.

So are you prepared? Are you ready to take on a little more responsibility to literally go *outside* of the current financial system, and potentially benefit huge as the future becomes the present?

Then follow me through the next section...

Buying Your First Bitcoin

Step #1 is to login to your Coinbase account.

To buy Bitcoin, you'll first need to send a picture of your government-issued ID. You can take a picture on your phone or use your computer's webcam. Once you send in this picture, it will take anywhere from minutes to days to verify depending on the method you used to send it in.

As soon as your ID is verified, you'll be able to buy crypto using a variety of methods. If you want to buy more than $300, you need to connect your bank account and go through a verification process.

If you'd like to start out small, you can use your credit card or PayPal account.

You can then choose how much you'd like to purchase. Type your amount in below:

Buy		Sell

Cryptocurrency

Bitcoin
BTC   @ $5,035.50

Payment Method

VISA

Amount

Weekly card limit $300.00 remaining · View limits

0.00   USD   ⇌   0.00   BTC

Repeat this buy   Daily   Weekly   Every two weeks   Monthly

Buy Bitcoin

When you're ready, click "Buy Bitcoin." If the purchase is successful, you'll get the below notification:

Your purchase was successful!

BTC will be available in your BTC Wallet instantly.

Invite your friends

Once your friend buys or sells $100 of cryptocurrency, you will both get $10 of free bitcoin.

View accounts   Start new buy

You can repeat the exact same process with Ethereum and Litecoin. Now, when you complete this process, the money goes into Coinbase, which means you're hosting it on an exchange. As I've mentioned, this is a dangerous place to keep your crypto. So let's move it to your Trust Wallet, which, hopefully, you've already set up.

Each coin you buy will need its own wallet within Trust. Don't worry, Trust makes it incredibly easy to manage it all. Within your wallet, click "Bitcoin." If you don't see Bitcoin, you'll need to add it manually using the search bar, like so:

(You'll have to use this same process when you add
Litecoin and Ethereum later.)

To transfer your Bitcoin from Coinbase to Trust, go to the
"Accounts" tab in Coinbase. Find Bitcoin, and push "send."
Then go into the Trust Wallet, Bitcoin, and push "receive."
You'll see the following screen:

‹ Back   **Bitcoin**   Buy   ◪

COIN

₿

0 BTC

$5,043.81 -4.95%

| ↑ Send | ↓ Receive |

Receiving address

bc1qvsehxuj88qapgskanzd5qypr52huukhd45cct9   ⧉

Today

(L) **Pending**   +0.0016 BTC
     From: bc1q7pd6w...s50wqusm3g32

🗔¹
Wallet   DApps   Settings

Click on your "receiving address" to copy it. This is your public key, which means it's safe to be shared. Paste it into the Coinbase "Bitcoin Address" field. Then type in how much crypto you want to send. Click the button "Use Max" to send all the BTC you have stored in your Coinbase account.

That's it! You should now see a "pending" transfer as shown in the previous image.

The process is the same on Coinbase for both Ethereum and Litecoin. But it's a little different with Trust. That's because you'll need separate public key addresses for each coin. Don't worry—it's very easy to find.

First, find your wallet on Trust by using the search function.

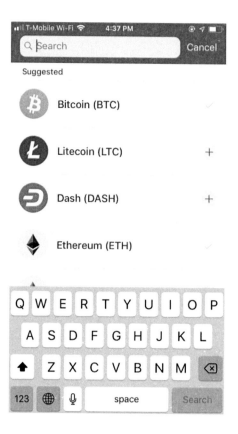

Then click on it and once again copy your "Receiving address." Paste it in on Coinbase and send the amount of crypto you want to send to your wallet.

And just like that, you now have all your crypto stored on your phone. And as a result, you can now access your crypto anywhere in the world if you've written down your mnemonic phrase (WHICH YOU ABSOLUTELY NEED TO DO!).

Tracking Your Crypto With Etherscan and Block Explorers

When you send your first crypto, you may notice something. There is a little bit of latency between when your crypto is sent, and when it actually arrives in the location you sent it to. This is called the "pucker moment", because in the early days of crypto, people would wonder if their money *really* would transfer. Although the technology was sound, sending money in this way and not knowing exactly where it is caused butterflies in a lot of people's stomachs.

The truth is, as long as you are using the correct public keys, sending crypto is extremely reliable. Still, you may be interested in knowing all the paths your crypto takes along the way.

As you know by now, one of the largest benefits of crypto is its transparency. You can see where it is. You can see where it's going. And you can see every single step in-between.

There are two tools you can use to do this. If you are tracking Bitcoin, you can use a variety of different websites that host "Bitcoin Block Explorers". Just Google this phrase and you will be shown several. I like the ones hosted by blockchain.com and live.blockcypher.com. If you're sending Ethereum or any of the other ERC-20 coins, you'll use a web app called Etherscan.

Using a Cold Storage Hardware Solution

Remember: Crypto has many different levels to it. And each level you move into brings more security, but also more responsibility. So far we've moved from Exchanges—the top level—into software wallets. Now, let's take it one step further and get you totally secured.

Although Software wallets are secure, and will most likely keep your crypto safe for life, as long as you're on a device connected to the Internet, you're at risk of a hack and getting your crypto stolen.

That's why the next level involves taking your coins and storing them in an offline device specifically designed to keep crypto safe. I'm talking about a "cold storage" device.

There are a few different companies that offer these solutions, but I'm going to recommend you use one called Ledger. Ledger is one of the most popular solutions, so it has the most security and support.

NOTE: It's important that you *only* buy Ledger through their website. Although they do have an Amazon store, if you buy on Amazon you may accidentally buy a compromised device from a third-party.

I will be pasting the basic instructions for setting up your Ledger Nano S from the Ledger support website. However, I encourage you to check out the support site for yourself, as they have tons of detailed, easy-to-follow instructions:

https://support.ledger.com

How to Set Up Your Ledger Wallet

Instructions pasted from support.ledger.com:

1. Connect the Ledger Nano S to your computer using the supplied USB cable.

2. Read the instructions on the screen. Press both buttons simultaneously to proceed.

3. Press the right button located above the validation icon when "Configure as new device?" is displayed.

Choose a Pin Code

*   Update Firmware to 1.41

*   Choose a PIN code between 4 and 8 digits long.

To set your PIN:

1. Press both buttons when Choose a PIN is displayed on the device.

2. Press the right or left button to choose the first digit of your PIN code.

3. Press both buttons to select the digit.

4. Repeat the process until all digits of your PIN code are selected.

5. Select the check icon (✓) and press both buttons to confirm the pincode.

Save Your Recovery Phrase

Your 24-word recovery phrase will now be displayed word by word on the Ledger Nano S screen. Be careful, your recovery phrase will be displayed only once.

1. Take the blank Recovery sheet supplied in the box.

2. Write down the first word (Word #1) on the Recovery sheet. Verify that you have copied it correctly in position 1.

3. Press the right button to move to the second word (Word #2). Write it in position 2 on the Recovery sheet. Verify that you've copied it correctly.

4. Repeat the process until the twenty-fourth word (Word #24). Confirm your recovery phrase will be shown on the screen after word 24.

5. Select the requested word by navigating with the left or right button. Validate the word by pressing both buttons. Repeat this step for each requested word.

6. Your device is now ready is shown once you've successfully completed the initialization.

Send and Receive Crypto With Ledger

Receive Crypto Assets

1. Click Receive on the left panel, or from the top of an account detail page.

2. Type or use the drop-down list to choose the account to receive crypto assets in.

3. Click Next.

4. Connect and unlock your Ledger Nano S. Then open the crypto asset app as instructed.

5. Read the on-screen instructions and click on Verify to generate a receive address on your device.

6. Verify that the address shown on your screen is the same as the address shown in Ledger Live. If the addresses are the same, press the right button on your device to confirm.

7. Click Copy to copy the address and share it with the sender of the transaction. Carefully check that the address does not change after you copy and paste it.

Don't have your device?

- On the account selection screen, click on I don't have my device to generate a receive address.

- The generated receive address does not benefit from the optimal level of security because the receive address on Ledger Live is not verified on your Ledger Nano S.

Send Crypto Assets

1. Click Send on the left panel.

2. Type or use the drop-down list to select the account to debit.

3. Enter the Recipient address. For optimal security, make sure always to double-check addresses that you copy and paste.

4. Enter the Amount of the crypto asset to send, or its countervalue*.

5. Choose the Network fees from the drop-down list. A higher fee leads to a faster processing of the transaction. Learn more...

6. Click Continue.

Verify and sign

1. Connect and unlock your Ledger Nano S.

2. Open the crypto asset app as instructed.

3. Click Continue.

4. Carefully verify all transaction details on your device.

5. Press the right button to confirm and sign the transaction if everything is correct. The transaction is then signed and sent to the network for confirmation.

6. Click View operation details to track the transaction until it gets confirmed.

Welcome to the Future

In writing this book, I wanted to light the fire. I wanted to inspire. I wanted to instruct. This book was not a dialogue between us, but a declaration. A shout to tell you why I'm so passionate about advocating for cryptocurrency. Even when—especially when—it might seem like the situation is very "bearish."

I've spoken to enough experts to see the crypto future coming years before it actually hits. I know where the industry is *most likely* going. And I want to make sure as many people as possible get on the train with me. Because the future is going to be absolutely incredible if we help guide it. And if you prepare like I've instructed you in this book, *you'll be ready to lead it with me.*

The kinds of changes that are coming in the future have never happened in the history of the human race! The opportunities that are coming are unlike anything we've ever seen before. I am writing this book so that I can, in good conscience, say that I TOLD everyone all I possibly could about what was going on. Whether you choose to act on it or not is up to you—at least I did what I knew I had to do.

I could tell you every logical reason I know for crypto. And, for the most part, in this book I have. But until you get the *emotional* impact this could *actually* have in your life starting today, you're not going to be excited about joining the movement.

I wrote this book to show you that we need to stick together and look at the bigger picture. We need to open up about the injustices and unfair practices that plague our society. We need to not be ashamed to speak up and demand change. And we need, most of all, to realize that the future is what we make it.

Now is the time where we have a fighting chance. Like any cliché movie with an underdog, the odds are against us. The people that would love to continue on the same path have more money, more influence, more power, and are better organized. But, we have humanity. We have our stories. And through these stories, we can see that our common goals are not too different.

I wrote this book to instruct you on the first steps in thinking about the possibilities of blockchain and cryptocurrency.

The freedom that can be captured if we can collectively reach out our hands and take it.

The economic benefits if we started thinking differently and looking to how this technology could be adapted for OUR benefit in the future.

This book, though sometimes a bit technical and like an instruction manual, was written in this way so that you can have the ideas, have the stories, and have the knowledge to start charging into the future with the rest of us. Because that is what we are! Underdogs fighting against a system that has controlled and managed us for our entire lives...*without any of our input.*

This is not an easy journey. You can't just download a crypto wallet and cure world hunger. This is the start of organizing something bigger than ourselves. This is the beginning of a revolution.

Why does the United States of America have the Second Amendment? It is to protect ourselves, as well as the tool of change. Well, I am telling you now that a new tool of change has arrived.

No, it does not shoot or blow things up. What it does is preserve sovereignty by giving us an unbreakable, unhackable, immutable, and uncensorable tool to protect our rights.

If the phrase "money is power" is true, then we will be in control of the greatest power the world has ever seen. We will be in control of our own money!

Freedom of speech: A freedom that has been trodden on more and more in the age of privatized social media, can be protected by blockchain technology and decentralized systems. I would rather allow all speech than try to figure out where it should be censored. Who draws this line? You? Me? Trump? Obama? The Pope?

The right to life, liberty, and the pursuit of happiness is constantly being chipped away by banks, taxes, interest rates, new laws with fees and taxes, corrupt government spending, rigged elections, murky election processes...the list could go on, but I think you get the point.

With control of our money and with voting on the blockchain, we could start to see real accountability that could lead to real change. But we need to pick up arms. No not guns, but blockchain.

Blockchain is the new weapon of this revolution. And by using this book to buy crypto, you've joined the biggest movement for change this world has ever seen.

Get Real-Time Updates on the Exact Coins We're Buying

I'd like to replace the whole page with this instead: Congratulations: You now have a basic knowledge of cryptocurrency. You know how it was invented. You know where it's at right now. And most importantly, you know where it's going.

The truth is, even though a fully-cryptofied world could be years away, there is tremendous value to be had right now, both from investing in and using it.

At CRYPTO 101 Insider, we're constantly told things off-the-air from founders who are excited to share their secrets with us. We know about many closed-door partnerships and new products before virtually anyone else hears about them. In the spirit of decentralization, we want to bring that same information to you.

If you're interested in joining the most cutting-edge crypto community on the planet—and learning about top coins WAY before they hit mainstream—join us as a Crypto 101 insider:

crypto101insider.com

Disclaimer

This book is presented solely for educational and entertainment purposes. The author and publisher are not offering it as legal, accounting, or other professional services advice. While best efforts have been used in preparing this book, the author and publisher make no representations or warranties of any kind and assume no liabilities of any kind with respect to the accuracy or completeness of the contents and specifically disclaim any implied warranties of merchantability or fitness of use for a particular purpose. Neither the author nor the publisher shall be held liable or responsible to any person or entity with respect to any loss or incidental or consequential damages caused, or alleged to have been caused, directly or indirectly, by the information contained herein. Any use of this information is at your own risk.

Citations

1. "Financial Health Network » U.S. Financial Health Pulse–Overview." https://finhealthnetwork.org/u-s-financial-health-pulse/. Accessed 22 May. 2019.
2. "Inequallty World report-World Inequality Report 2018." https://wir2018.wid.world/files/download/wlr2018-summary-english.pdf. Accessed 22 May. 2019.
3. "Average Student Loan Debt in the U.S.-2019 Statistics ...-Nitro College." https://www.nitrocollege.com/research/average-student-loan-debt. Accessed 22 May. 2019.
4. "Bitcoin price drop: what a crypto evangelist thinks about its terrible 2018.." 28 Dec. 2018, https://slate.com/technology/2018/12/bitcoin-price-cryptocurrency-bubble-burst.html. Accessed 22 May. 2019.
5. "Tulips · University of Minnesota Libraries." https://www.lib.umn.edu/bell/tradeproducts/tulips. Accessed 22 May. 2019.
6. "BBC-Culture-Tulip mania: The flowers that cost more than houses." 3 May. 2016, http://www.bbc.com/culture/story/20160419-tulip-mania-the-flowers-that-cost-more-than-houses. Accessed 22 May. 2019.
7. "A Brief History of Go | American Go Association." https://www.usgo.org/brief-history-go. Accessed 22 May. 2019.
8. "Why Google AI game Go is harder than chess-Business Insider." 10 Mar. 2016, https://www.businessinsider.com/why-google-ai-game-go-is-harder-than-chess-2016-3. Accessed 22 May. 2019.
9. "Computers Are Great at Chess, But That Doesn't Mean the Game Is ...." 10 Feb. 2017, https://www.smithsonianmag.com/

smart-news/what-first-man-lose-computer-said-about-
chess-21st-century-180962046/. Accessed 22 May. 2019.

10. "How Google's AlphaGo Beat Lee Sedol, a Go World ...- The
Atlantic." 28 Mar. 2016, https://www.theatlantic.com/technology/
archive/2016/03/the-invisible-opponent/475611/. Accessed 22
May. 2019.

11. "AlphaGo returns upgraded, wins 60 straight games online |
ZDNet." 5 Jan. 2017, https://www.zdnet.com/article/alphago-
returns-upgraded-wins-60-straight-games-online/. Accessed 22
May. 2019.

12. "Facebook's artificial intelligence robots shut down ...- The
Independent." 31 Jul. 2017, https://www.independent.co.uk/life-
style/gadgets-and-tech/news/Facebook-artificial-intelligence-ai-
chatbot-new-language-research-openai-google-a7869706.html.
Accessed 23 May. 2019.

13. "Facebook AI Creates Its Own Language In Creepy Preview
Of Our ...." 31 Jul. 2017, https://www.forbes.com/sites/
tonybradley/2017/07/31/Facebook-ai-creates-its-own-language-
in-creepy-preview-of-our-potential-future/. Accessed 22 May.
2019.

14. "Filing: OxyContin maker forecast 'blizzard of prescriptions'-
AP News." 15 Jan. 2019, https://www.apnews.com/
4e2da888ede44c3db129b46d76504778. Accessed 22 May.
2019.

15. "OxyContin-pusher Purdue blames everyone but itself for
opioid crisis ...." 6 Mar. 2019, https://arstechnica.com/science/
2019/03/oxycontin-pusher-purdue-blames-everyone-but-itself-
for-opioid-crisis/. Accessed 22 May. 2019.

16. "How AI can be a force for good | Science." https://
science.sciencemag.org/content/361/6404/751. Accessed 22
May. 2019.

17. "Declining birth rate in Developed Countries: A radical policy re ...- NCBI." https://www.ncbi.nlm.nih.gov/pmc/articles/PMC4255510/. Accessed 22 May. 2019.

18. "Near-Earth Asteroid Mining-Semantic Scholar." 14 Dec. 2001, https://pdfs.semanticscholar.org/e444/0ba004c28f88a698aa8f08635d5f39187f62.pdf. Accessed 22 May. 2019.

19. "Timeline: When and how Elon Musk, SpaceX plan to populate Mars ...." 14 Oct. 2018, https://www.businessinsider.com/elon-musk-spacex-mars-plan-timeline-2018-10. Accessed 22 May. 2019.

20. "Elon Musk: 'Paper money is going away,' cryptocurrency tech has merit." 20 Feb. 2019, https://www.cnbc.com/2019/02/20/elon-musk-paper-money-is-going-away-cryptocurrency-tech-has-merit.html. Accessed 22 May. 2019.

21. "As He Clips Our Coins, Bernanke Steals A Page From Nero's Playbook." 25 Sep. 2013, https://www.forbes.com/sites/realspin/2013/09/25/as-he-clips-our-coins-bernanke-steals-a-page-from-neros-playbook/. Accessed 22 May. 2019.

22. "What Happens to Bitcoin After All 21 Million Are Mined?-Investopedia." 8 May. 2019, https://www.investopedia.com/tech/what-happens-bitcoin-after-21-million-mined/. Accessed 22 May. 2019.

23. "The Operation and Demise of the Bretton Woods ...- Naked Capitalism." 25 Apr. 2017, https://www.nakedcapitalism.com/2017/04/operation-demise-bretton-woods-system-1958-1971.html. Accessed 22 May. 2019.

24. "Fractional Reserve Banking-Investopedia." 17 Jan. 2019, https://www.investopedia.com/terms/f/fractionalreservebanking.asp. Accessed 22 May. 2019.

25. "What Is a DDA Bank Account? | Pocketsense." https://pocketsense.com/dda-bank-account-1711.html. Accessed 22 May. 2019.

26. "Time deposit Definition | Bankrate.com." https://www.bankrate.com/glossary/t/time-deposit/. Accessed 22 May. 2019.

27. "Creating Money | Boundless Economics-Lumen Learning." https://courses.lumenlearning.com/boundless-economics/chapter/creating-money/. Accessed 22 May. 2019.

28. "The Fed Is Not Printing Money, It's Doing Something Much Worse." 9 Mar. 2014, https://www.forbes.com/sites/johntamny/2014/03/09/the-fed-is-not-printing-money-its-doing-something-much-worse/. Accessed 22 May. 2019.

29. "Government-Historical Debt Outstanding-Annual ...-TreasuryDirect." 12 Oct. 2018, https://www.treasurydirect.gov/govt/reports/pd/histdebt/histdebt_histo5.htm. Accessed 23 May. 2019.

30. "Dollar Value Today: Why It's Less, Who Keeps Track-The Balance." 13 May. 2019, https://www.thebalance.com/what-is-the-value-of-a-dollar-today-3306105. Accessed 22 May. 2019.

31. "Banks Crushed Profit Record With $237 Billion in 2018, FDIC Says ...." 21 Feb. 2019, https://www.bloomberg.com/news/articles/2019-02-21/banks-crushed-profit-record-with-237-billion-in-2018-fdic-says. Accessed 22 May. 2019.

32. "The top frauds of 2018 | Consumer Information." 28 Feb. 2019, https://www.consumer.ftc.gov/blog/2019/02/top-frauds-2018. Accessed 22 May. 2019.

33. "Facts + Statistics: Identity theft and cybercrime | III." https://www.iii.org/fact-statistic/facts-statistics-identity-theft-and-cybercrime. Accessed 22 May. 2019.

34. "Report: Google Uses About 900,000 Servers | Data Center Knowledge." 1 Aug. 2011, https://www.datacenterknowledge.com/archives/2011/08/01/report-google-uses-about-900000-servers. Accessed 22 May. 2019.

35. "A brief history of money-IEEE Journals & Magazine-IEEE Xplore." 24 May. 2012, https://ieeexplore.ieee.org/document/6203967/. Accessed 22 May. 2019.

36. "Venezuelan streets quiet after currency devaluation-Reuters." 21 Aug. 2018, https://www.reuters.com/article/us-venezuela-economy/venezuelan-streets-quiet-after-currency-devaluation-idUSKCN1L61E4. Accessed 22 May. 2019.

37. "Human Development Report 2014-Human Development Reports." http://hdr.undp.org/en/content/human-development-report-2014. Accessed 22 May. 2019.

38. "Nokia crosses one-billion mark-Engadget." 21 Sep. 2005, https://www.engadget.com/2005/09/21/nokia-crosses-one-billion-mark/. Accessed 22 May. 2019.

39. "Sending Money Home-Remittances Gateway." https://www.remittancesgateway.org/wp-content/uploads/2017/12/2017-06-14_SendingMoneyHome_WEB-2.pdf. Accessed 22 May. 2019.

40. "World's Largest Hedge Fund Founder: Bitcoin is a 'Bubble'-CoinDesk." 19 Sep. 2017, https://www.coindesk.com/bridgewater-associates-head-says-bitcoin-bubble. Accessed 22 May. 2019.

41. "Bitcoin Is Evil-Paul Krugman-The New York Times." 28 Dec. 2013, https://krugman.blogs.nytimes.com/2013/12/28/bitcoin-is-evil/. Accessed 22 May. 2019.

42. "Bill Gates: cryptocurrencies have 'caused deaths in a fairly direct way ...." 28 Feb. 2018, https://www.theguardian.com/

technology/2018/feb/28/bill-gates-cryptocurrencies-deaths-bitcoin-steve-wozniak-scam. Accessed 22 May. 2019.

43. "Warren Buffett Urges Investors to 'Stay Away' from Bitcoin-CoinDesk." 14 Mar. 2014, https://www.coindesk.com/warren-buffett-investors-stay-away-bitcoin. Accessed 22 May. 2019.

44. "Wolf of Wall Street Jordan Belfort Thinks There Are Bitcoin Scams A ...." 30 Aug. 2018, https://blockonomi.com/jordan-belfort-bitcoin-scams/. Accessed 22 May. 2019.

45. "Don't buy bitcoin, says wealth manager Peter Mallouk-CNBC.com." 3 Apr. 2019, https://www.cnbc.com/2019/04/02/dont-buy-bitcoin-says-wealth-manager-peter-mallouk.html. Accessed 22 May. 2019.

46. "JP Morgan is rolling out the first US bank-backed cryptocurrency." 14 Feb. 2019, https://www.cnbc.com/2019/02/13/jp-morgan-is-rolling-out-the-first-us-bank-backed-cryptocurrency-to-transform-payments--.html. Accessed 22 May. 2019.

47. "Thomas A. Edison quote: Fooling around with alternating currents is ...." https://www.azquotes.com/quote/766478. Accessed 22 May. 2019.

48. "Horace Rackham-Wikipedia." https://en.wikipedia.org/wiki/Horace_Rackham. Accessed 22 May. 2019.

49. "Here Are A Few Things That Even Einstein Got Wrong | IFLScience." 17 Mar. 2018, https://www.iflscience.com/physics/here-are-a-few-things-that-even-einstein-got-wrong/page-2/. Accessed 22 May. 2019.

50. "Top 10 worst tech predictions of all time | ZDNet." 1 Jan. 2008, https://www.zdnet.com/article/top-10-worst-tech-predictions-of-all-time/. Accessed 22 May. 2019.

51. "Steve Jobs: Rolling Stone's 2003 Interview–Rolling Stone." 6 Oct. 2011, https://www.rollingstone.com/culture/culture-news/

steve-jobs-rolling-stones-2003-interview-243284/. Accessed 22 May. 2019.

52. "Ballmer: iPhone has "no chance" of gaining significant market share ...." 30 Apr. 2007, https://arstechnica.com/information-technology/2007/04/ballmer-says-iphone-has-no-chance-to-gain-significant-market-share/. Accessed 22 May. 2019.

53. "Fidelity Is Launching a Crypto Trading Platform-CoinDesk." 15 Oct. 2018, https://www.coindesk.com/fidelity-reveals-cryptocurrency-and-digital-asset-trading-platform. Accessed 22 May. 2019.

54. "SEC Launches New Strategic Hub for Innovation and Financial ...." 18 Oct. 2018, https://www.sec.gov/news/press-release/2018-240. Accessed 22 May. 2019.

55. "Goldman Sachs CFO calls speculation about bitcoin 'fake news'." 6 Sep. 2018, https://www.cnbc.com/2018/09/06/goldman-sachs-cfo-calls-reports-of-shutting-down-crypto-desk-fake-news.html. Accessed 22 May. 2019.

56. "NYSE Operator Announces New Global Digital Assets Platform, Plans ...." 3 Aug. 2018, https://cointelegraph.com/news/nyse-operator-announces-new-global-digital-assets-platform-plans-bitcoin-futures-launch. Accessed 22 May. 2019.

57. "AmEx Upgrades Rewards Program with Hyperledger Blockchain ...." 23 May. 2018, https://www.coindesk.com/american-express-upgrades-rewards-program-hyperledger-blockchain. Accessed 22 May. 2019.

58. "Oracle Blockchain Opens for Business | Fortune." http://fortune.com/2018/07/16/oracle-blockchain-available/. Accessed 22 May. 2019.

59. "Tencent Drives China's Tech Hub to a Blockchain Future | CryptoSlate." 30 May. 2018, https://cryptoslate.com/tencent-

drives-chinas-tech-hub-to-a-blockchain-future/. Accessed 22 May. 2019.

60. "Alibaba Affiliate to Boost Blockchain Development After $14 Billion ...." 8 Jun. 2018, https://www.coindesk.com/alibaba-affiliate-to-boost-blockchain-development-after-14-billion-raise. Accessed 22 May. 2019.

61. "Facebook Coin Could Drive a 'Mass-Adoption' of Crypto, Study ...." 16 May. 2019, https://bitcoinist.com/Facebook-coin-stablecoin-crypto-mass-adoption/. Accessed 22 May. 2019.

62. "cryptocurrency Trading | TD Ameritrade." https://www.tdameritrade.com/investment-products/cryptocurrency-trading.page. Accessed 22 May. 2019.

63. "ConsenSys partners with Amazon Web Services for blockchain ...." 10 Nov. 2018, https://cryptonewsreview.com/consensys-partners-with-amazon-web-services-for-blockchain-marketplace-kaleido/. Accessed 22 May. 2019.

64. "Nestle, Walmart, Unilever, Kroger Might Be First Grocery Giants To ...." 2 May. 2019, https://www.investinblockchain.com/nestle-walmart-unilever-kroger-first-grocery-giants-to-fully-use-blockchain-tech-by-2025-says-gartner-reports/. Accessed 23 May. 2019.

65. "Pfizer And Others Join Working Group To Use Blockchain Protocol For ...." 2 May. 2019, https://www.forbes.com/sites/rachelwolfson/2019/05/02/pfizer-and-other-healthcare-companies-aim-to-bring-blockchain-based-chargeback-protocol-to-market/. Accessed 23 May. 2019.

66. "Anheuser-Busch Owner Pilots Blockchain for Shipping-CoinDesk." 15 Mar. 2018, https://www.coindesk.com/anheuser-busch-owner-pilots-blockchain-shipping. Accessed 23 May. 2019.

67. "Google Is Working On Blockchain-Related Technology." https://www.bloombergquint.com/technology/google-is-said-to-work-on-its-own-blockchain-related-technology. Accessed 23 May. 2019.

68. "Chinese ICOs: China bans fundraising through initial coin offerings ...." 4 Sep. 2017, https://www.cnbc.com/2017/09/04/chinese-icos-china-bans-fundraising-through-initial-coin-offerings-report-says.html. Accessed 22 May. 2019.

69. "Japan decides bitcoin is not a currency-MarketWatch." 7 Mar. 2014, https://www.marketwatch.com/story/japan-decides-bitcoin-is-not-a-currency-2014-03-07. Accessed 22 May. 2019.

70. "Japan Officially Recognizes Bitcoin and Digital Currencies as Money." 2 May. 2016, https://cointelegraph.com/news/japan-officially-recognizes-bitcoin-and-digital-currencies-as-money. Accessed 22 May. 2019.

71. "India's central bank bans financial firms from dealing with cryptocurrency." 5 Apr. 2018, https://www.cnbc.com/2018/04/05/indias-central-bank-bans-financial-firms-from-dealing-with-cryptocurrency.html. Accessed 22 May. 2019.

72. "SEC.gov | Spotlight on Initial Coin Offerings (ICOs)." 11 Apr. 2019, https://www.sec.gov/ICO. Accessed 22 May. 2019.

73. "Virtual Currencies | Internal Revenue Service." https://www.irs.gov/businesses/small-businesses-self-employed/virtual-currencies. Accessed 22 May. 2019.

74. "US Could Put Crypto Wallets on OFAC Sanctions List-CoinDesk." 21 Mar. 2018, https://www.coindesk.com/treasury-department-says-to-not-transact-with-rogue-nations-crypto-users. Accessed 22 May. 2019.

75. "FinCEN Issues Guidance on Virtual Currencies and Regulatory ...." 18 Mar. 2013, https://www.fincen.gov/news/news-

releases/fincen-issues-guidance-virtual-currencies-and-regulatory-responsibilities. Accessed 22 May. 2019.

76. "Bitcoin and ether are not securities, but some initial coin offerings may ...." 14 Jun. 2018, https://www.cnbc.com/2018/06/14/bitcoin-and-ethereum-are-not-securities-but-some-cryptocurrencies-may-be-sec-official-says.html. Accessed 22 May. 2019.

77. "Bitcoin Will Hit $1 Million in 2020 Because Maths, Stupid: John McAfee." 17 Apr. 2019, https://www.ccn.com/john-mcafee-maths-bitcoin-1-million-by-2020. Accessed 22 May. 2019.

78. "Financial Inclusion on the Rise, But Gaps Remain, Global Findex ...." https://www.worldbank.org/en/news/press-release/2018/04/19/financial-inclusion-on-the-rise-but-gaps-remain-global-findex-database-shows. Accessed 22 May. 2019.

79. "About-Coinbase." https://www.Coinbase.com/about. Accessed 23 May. 2019.

80. "$2 Million Allegedly Stolen From Cryptocurrency Vlogger in ...- Gizmodo." 16 Apr. 2018, https://gizmodo.com/2-million-allegedly-stolen-from-cryptocurrency-vlogger-1825290362. Accessed 22 May. 2019.

81. "Yahoo Admits 500 Million Hit In 2014 Breach -- UPDATED-Forbes." 22 Sep. 2016, https://www.forbes.com/sites/thomasbrewster/2016/09/22/yahoo-500-million-hacked-by-nation-state/. Accessed 22 May. 2019.

82. "Encryption-1 Difference between symmetric and ...- Course Hero." https://www.coursehero.com/file/15328429/Encryption/. Accessed 22 May. 2019.

83. "The History of the Mt Gox Hack: Bitcoin's Biggest Heist-Blockonomi." https://blockonomi.com/mt-gox-hack/. Accessed 22 May. 2019.

84. "Equifax breaks down just how bad last year's data breach ...- NBC News." 8 May. 2018, https://www.nbcnews.com/news/us-news/equifax-breaks-down-just-how-bad-last-year-s-data-n872496. Accessed 22 May. 2019.

85. "Facebook fined for data breaches in Cambridge Analytica scandal ...." 11 Jul. 2018, https://www.theguardian.com/technology/2018/jul/11/Facebook-fined-for-data-breaches-in-cambridge-analytica-scandal. Accessed 22 May. 2019.

86. "FDIC: Weekly National Rates and Rate ...." 29 May. 2009, https://www.fdic.gov/regulations/resources/rates/. Accessed 22 May. 2019.

87. "erc 20-How many Ethereum-based tokens are there?- Ethereum ...." 28 Nov. 2017, https://ethereum.stackexchange.com/questions/31922/how-many-ethereum-based-tokens-are-there. Accessed 22 May. 2019.

88. "Litecoin hits a record high and is up nearly 1400 percent ...- CNBC.com." 29 Aug. 2017, https://www.cnbc.com/2017/08/29/litcoin-price-hits-record-high.html. Accessed 22 May. 2019.

89. "Chainanalysis- 3.8 million Bitcoin is lost forever–Steemit." https://steemit.com/cryptocurrency/@crypto-z/chainanalysis-3-8-million-bitcoin-is-lost-forever. Accessed 22 May. 2019.

90. "$400 Million Missing In Hack Of Japanese Digital Currency Exchange ...." 26 Jan. 2018, https://www.npr.org/sections/thetwo-way/2018/01/26/581130968/-400-million-missing-in-hack-of-japanese-digital-currency-exchange. Accessed 22 May. 2019.

91. "About-Coinbase." https://www.Coinbase.com/about. Accessed 22 May. 2019.

92. "A behind the scenes look at the biggest (and quietest) crypto transfer ...." 19 Dec. 2018, https://blog.Coinbase.com/a-behind-the-scenes-look-at-the-biggest-and-quietest-crypto-transfer-on-record-682ff4a6d9e4. Accessed 22 May. 2019.

93. "QuadrigaCX CEO Lost $190 Million in Crypto, Former Friend Says He ...." 19 Apr. 2019, https://www.newsbtc.com/2019/04/19/quadrigacx-ceo-lost-190-million-in-crypto-former-friend-says-he-was-fearful/. Accessed 22 May. 2019.

Contributions:

Kevin Stanley
Michael Collins
Jennifer Perez
Jeromy Green